T0209294

NEW CREATION
THINKING
Living Life from the Inside Out

WAYNE KNIFFEN

WESTBOW
PRESS®
A DIVISION OF THOMAS NELSON
& ZONDERVAN

WestBow Press books may be ordered through booksellers or by contacting:

WestBow Press
A Division of Thomas Nelson & Zondervan
1663 Liberty Drive
Bloomington, IN 47403
www.westbowpress.com
844-714-3454

ISBN: 978-1-6642-8924-6 (sc)
ISBN: 978-1-6642-8923-9 (hc)
ISBN: 978-1-6642-8925-3 (e)

Library of Congress Control Number: 2023900642

Print information available on the last page.

WestBow Press rev. date: 1/20/2023

To all the incredible mentors who have contributed to my spiritual growth by their willingness to spend time with me. Your insight, encouragement, sacrifice of time, and, most of all, your patience have helped me become who I am today—madly in love with my Lord and Savior, Jesus Christ. A special thank you to two men who are now in the Lord's presence: Dr. (Brother Johnny) John H. Beard and Lewis Bell. These two men will always have a special place in my memory and in my heart.

CONTENTS

INTRODUCTION

It takes spunk and a lot of moxie to walk away from being an average Christian. Most Christians have settled for a life that is far beneath their identities as new creations in Christ. They have forfeited today for a tomorrow that will never get here. Today is yesterday's tomorrow. If tomorrow does get here, it will be our today.

The majority of those who have had a born-from-above experience with Christ have settled for a life that does not measure up to the new creation identities they have been gifted with. They live with a *someday mentality*. "Someday, I'll have victory over my temper." "I'll be happy someday." "Someday, I'll be at peace." "I'll have victory over that besetting sin someday; if not today, I will—someday."

As my friend John O'Brian says, "Most Christians live with a distance-and-delay mentality." Those who have this perspective believe that everything God has provided for us in Christ has been deposited in our personal heavenly bank accounts. These birthright privileges may belong to us now, but we can't access or appropriate them until we get to heaven—someday. We lack a *now perspective*, and this is our spiritual Achilles' heel. This is why the casualty rate is so high within the community of faith. The anthem hymn for the church has been "I'll Fly Away," which was written by Albert E. Brumley in 1929. The third stanza is the church's favorite. They will sing it with gusto: "Just a few more weary days, and then I'll fly away." A few more weary days, and then—someday.

What we have is a thinking problem. Even though we have become new creations in Christ, we still think like we did before we knew Him. We may have our tickets to heaven punched, but between now and then, we're in survival mode. If we can just make it through a few more weary days, life will be better. There is a huge difference between being alive and living life.

Existing is not what God had in mind when He exchanged our old lives for new ones. He made us to be more than conquerors through Him (Romans 8:37 NKJV). God always leads us in triumph in Christ (2 Corinthians 2:14 NKJV). If we were created to be overcomers while we live in this world, then why are so many Christians being overcome by the world? I contend it's because we don't think like the new creations we have become in Christ. Most have settled for lives that are mediocre at best.

Far too many within the community of faith are satisfied with being average. What is wrong with being average? Doesn't it mean the same thing as normal? I believe most of us want people to think we are normal. Mull over this definition of average: Average is to be the best of the worst and worst of the best. Do you still want to be normal? Christians who have settled for being normal are really subnormal. This is why so many in the community of faith perceive Christians who are expressing their faith in a normal fashion as abnormal. We have become comfortable with being average. Could the following statement from Leonard Ravenhill adequately define Christianity today? "Christianity today is so subnormal that if any Christian began to act like a normal New Testament Christian, they would be considered abnormal." This statement is as true today as it was when it was spoken. Being subnormal has become the new normal.

We are creatures of comfort. We like familiarity. Most of us are resistant to anything that threatens our status quo. This includes having our theological grids challenged. We have become comfortable with what we believe, and we are very reluctant to open ourselves up to something that might require a shift in our belief system, especially if it threatens what we have embraced for any period of time. New creation thinking does just that. It forces us to expand the parameters of our spiritual thinking. This makes us very reluctant to kick over the traces. We fear we might lose control (like we have ever been in control) and appear weird or even foolish to other believers, as well as unbelievers.

> When we tell you these things, we do not use words that come from human wisdom. Instead, we speak words given to us by the Spirit, using the Spirit's words to explain spiritual truths. But people who aren't spiritual can't receive these truths from God's Spirit. It all sounds foolish to them and they can't understand it, for only those who are spiritual can understand what the Spirit means. *Those who are spiritual can evaluate all things,* but they themselves cannot be evaluated by others. "For, Who can know the Lord's thoughts? Who knows enough to teach Him?" But we understand these things, for *we have the mind of Christ.* (1 Corinthians 2:13–16 NLT, emphasis added)

Do we have the mind of Christ? We do if we are new creations. New creation thinking is not something that happens automatically, and it is not easy to do. It requires purposeful practice on our part. But it will be well worth the effort.

Here's what my good pastor friend, Dorman Duggan, says about truth: "Our first response to truth is usually resistance." Why is that? Because truth is like a finger that constantly pokes our comfort zones. And we don't like for our comfort zones to be disturbed, especially if they are in our belief systems.

Prayerfully, the Holy Spirit will use this book, *New Creation Thinking,* to do just that. It's a new day when how we think begins to line up with who we are as new creations in Christ. We will be alive, and we will begin to live for the first time. It will take faith and a whole lot of courage to walk away from being an average Christian:

Therefore, if anyone is in Christ, *he is a new creation*; old things have passed away; behold, all things have become new. (2 Corinthians 5:17 NKJV, emphasis added)

It's time to start thinking like the new creations we have become in Christ. This will only happen when we start living our lives from the inside out.

CHAPTER 1

LIVING LIFE FROM THE INSIDE OUT

———

There are only two ways life can be lived. Life is lived from the outside in or from the inside out. Most of us have chosen option number one: from the outside in. Before we accepted Christ as our Lord and Savior, this was our only option. We had no choice because we were wholly self-conscious in our natural selves. This self-focused condition was passed on to us through the corrupted seed of Adam.

The first Adam was created with a God focus. This is why he was not ashamed of his nakedness. His sin of disobedience moved him from being Spirit conscious (living life from the inside out) to being self-conscious (living life from the outside in). From that point forward, every person has been born with an outside-inside perspective on life. Adam's fall affected all of humanity. The purpose for Jesus coming to the earth and sacrificing His life for all of humankind was to give us the opportunity to be born again (born from above) and to move us from being self-conscious to being Spirit conscious. We now have the ability to live life from the inside out.

The Only Way a Dead Person Can Live

The instructions God gave to Adam about eating from the tree of the knowledge of good and evil were not ambiguous in any shape, form, or fashion:

> But *the Lord warned him*, "You may freely eat the fruit of every tree in the garden—except the tree of the knowledge of good and evil. *If you eat its fruit, you are sure to die.*" (Genesis 2:16–17 NLT, emphasis added)

God made sure Adam knew that if he disobeyed by eating from the forbidden tree, he would die. It did not say "maybe" die or "could" die; he would "surely" die. Adam did not listen to God's warning. Giving in to Satan's lie, he ate from the verboten tree.

There is something very conspicuous in this Genesis passage that is easily overlooked if we read it too fast. To my own chagrin, I read this passage for years but failed to notice what it says:

> At that moment (when they took a bite of the forbidden fruit) *their eyes were opened,* and they suddenly felt shame at their nakedness. So they sowed fig leaves together to cover themselves. (Genesis 3:7 NLT, emphasis added)

Their eyes opened? Did God create Adam and Eve without sight? Of course, He didn't. If God had created them blind, the warning He gave not to eat from the tree of the knowledge of good and evil would be irrelevant because they would not have been able to see what they were told to leave alone. That would not be good.

It is obvious that God was pleased with everything He created. After He brought the world into ordered existence by His spoken word, He said, "It is good" (Genesis 1:10 NKJV). He repeated this five times: "It is good." After Adam had been formed from the dust of the ground and given life, God said, "It is very good" (Genesis 1:31 NKJV). What is good or very good about not being able to see?

Before Adam sinned, he lived with a spirit consciousness. He lived his life from the inside out. His spirit received instructions from God, and he lived his life accordingly. This is how humanity was designed to live—from the inside out. Adam and Eve were naked, but they felt no shame because they were clothed in the glory of God (Genesis 2:25 NLT). Since they were created with the ability to see themselves the way God saw them, their focus was not on the external. There was no shame. Their identities were given to them by their Creator. It was not something they earned by their good works. Humanity was created to live life from the inside out—to live with God consciousness and not self-consciousness.

Adam and Eve's disobedience had eternal consequences for them and for the entire human race. Sin corrupted Adam's seed, and his iniquitous nature has been passed on to all of humanity. His sin also tainted all of creation. Adam's sin took him from being spirit focused to being self-focused. His spiritual eyes immediately closed the moment he disobeyed God's Word. The first thing Adam and Eve saw in their self-conscious state was their nakedness. They felt shame and covered themselves with fig leaves in an attempt to hide their guilt. Then they tried to conceal themselves from the presence of God. Before they succumbed to temptation, they saw themselves clothed in the glory of God because they were living as they were created to live—from the inside out.

God did not kill Adam for disobeying Him; death did. His sin gave life to death, and death took life from him. Adam is now living from the outside in; this is the only way a dead man can live. His spirit is dead, which negates his ability to comprehend the things of the Spirit. He receives his instructions from the world and lives accordingly. Don't forget Adam's sin corrupted the entire world. When we get our cues for how to live our lives from the world, we are getting our information from a perverted source. Death begets death. In Adam, all die (1 Corinthians 15:22 NLT).

Adam went from conversing with God face-to-face to hiding from God in disgrace. His spiritual condition had changed. God warned him about what would happen if he disobeyed and ate from the forbidden tree. Adam and Eve knew what God knew would happen if they ate from this tree. Their lives would be forever changed. No longer would it be possible for humanity to live life from the inside out: spirit consciousness. The human race is relegated to living life based on the principles the world considers moral and upright, which has become a contaminated source because of sin. Living life from the outside in is the only way a spiritually dead person can live.

God removed Adam and Eve from the garden of Eden, making it impossible for them to ever return. Their decision to disobey God removed them from the environment they were created to survive and thrive in—God Himself. The future of humankind appears to be hopeless. The tree of life has the power to impart life to the dead, but access to this tree has been blocked. And never forget that when God closes a door, no one can open it (Revelation 3:7 NLT). It seems that God's experiment with humanity has been a dismal failure. The only way for the dead to live again is for God to take life out of death.

Jesus Is the Only Way a Dead Person Can Live Again

Every person who has ever been born, is being born, or will be born bears the corrupted seed of the first Adam. His sin affected the entire human race—as well as all of creation. We did not inherit Adam's sin, but we did inherit his sinful nature (Romans 5:12 NKJV). The first Adam exchanged life for death when he chose to disobey God by eating from the forbidden tree.

The law of seed bearing after its own kind was established by God in the very beginning of time (Genesis 1:11 NKJV). Corrupted seed cannot produce incorruptible fruit any more than a cat can bark or a dog can meow. It's not in the nature of a cat to bark or a dog to meow. Seed determines their nature:

> When Adam sinned, sin entered the world. *Adam's*
> *sin brought death*, so death spread to everyone, for
> everyone sinned. (Romans 5:12 NLT, emphasis
> added)

Let's slow-walk our way through what Paul says in this verse. Before Adam sinned, death had no life. We could say it this way: death was created dead. Adam's sin is what put life into death. Once death had life, it took his life. Death was passed on to the entire human race:

> And as it is appointed for men to die once, but after
> this the judgment. (Hebrews 9:27 NKJV)

Death has been passed on to the entire human race—one per person.

God made it impossible for humanity to reenter the garden—so they could not eat the fruit from the tree of life. If this had been possible, the entire human race would be eternally separated from God with no hope of ever being reconciled. You and I are included in this equation:

> For *everyone* has sinned; *we all* fall short of God's
> glorious standard. (Romans 3:23 NLT, emphasis
> added)

Here's the good news. When Jesus died, death died. God took life out of death for those who will believe and for those who accept Jesus's offer of eternal life. For a child of God, death has no sting, and the grave has no victory (1 Corinthians 15:55 NKJV). How can this be? There is no life in death for a child of God. This new creation life is available to anyone and everyone. Anyone is welcome to come and drink of the water of life (Revelation 22:17 KJV).

For a dead person to have life, there must be a seed exchange. The corrupted seed that put life into death—then passed on to all of humanity by Adam—must be exchanged for incorruptible seed that produces life. This life seed is only available through Jesus Christ. The same verse that says, "In Adam, all die," also says, "*In Christ, all shall live*" (1 Corinthians 15:22 NKJV, emphasis added):

> For you have been born again, (from above) but not to a life that will quickly end. Your *new life* (new creation life) will last forever because it comes from the eternal, living word of God. (1 Peter 1:23 NLT, emphasis added)

Having been born of incorruptible seed, death has no life for the child of God.

Jesus is the Living Word:

> In the beginning the Word (Jesus) already existed. The Word (Jesus) was with God, and the Word (Jesus) was God. (John 1:1 NLT, emphasis added)

> So the Word (Jesus) became human and made his home among us. He was full of unfailing love and faithfulness. And we have seen his glory, the glory of the Father's one and only Son. (John 1:14 NLT, emphasis added).

God brought hope to a hopeless world when He sent His Son, Jesus Christ. Jesus came into this physical realm to make an exchange—to exchange death for life. His sinless obedience gives life to the dead. This is the glorious good news of the Gospel. It is not that Jesus lived and died; it is that He died and now lives. He is willing to give this resurrection life as a gift to anyone who will ask and receive it by faith. Jesus is the only way a dead person can live.

We Are New Creations in Christ

Everyone who belongs to Christ has been given a new life (2 Corinthians 5:17 NKJV). This new life we have received from the Lord gives us the ability to live our lives from the inside out: the way God intended from the very beginning.

From reading Genesis 3:24, it appears as if humanity's situation is hopeless, but God had a plan all along (Revelation 13:8 NLT). There's one thing we need to keep in mind. When God shuts a door, we need to be looking for the door He is opening. We also need to remember that when God opens a door, no one is able to shut it (Revelation 3:8 NKJV).

The door to the tree of life in the Garden of Eden was closed by God. That door cannot be opened by humanity, but God opened another door that made Him accessible to all of us. God brought to humanity what humanity could not return to: the environment for life. By God wrapping Himself up in the person of Jesus Christ, a way was made for humanity to exchange the fruit from the tree of the knowledge of good and evil (death) for the fruit from the tree of life (life). This is what salvation is all about. It is the exchange of death for life. These new creation lives that were gifted to us when we accepted and received Jesus Christ as our Lord and Savior are designed to be lived from the inside out. What the first Adam forfeited by his disobedience, the last Adam restored by His obedience. When we respond to the Lord's invitation to life, He moves us from being self-conscious to being Spirit conscious. As new creations in Christ, we now have a choice in how we live our lives.

When God restores us to Himself—the only environment for our survival—it frees us to have a choice. We can choose to live by the Spirit or live by the flesh. We will not be forced to do either. Since we have been endowed with free will, this decision belongs to us. Before we had our born-from-above experience with Christ, we did not have an alternative because we bore the corruptible seed of Adam. Death was in his seed, and death was passed on to the entire human race. Dead people do not have the ability to make choices. The only way we could live before Christ was by the flesh—from the outside in. Since we have become new creations in Christ, we need to start living like it. This begins by thinking like the new creations we have become.

What Does Living Inside Out Look Like?

Christ is not just the forgiver of our sins; He is our life (Colossians 3:4 NKJV). Luke tells us in the book of Acts, "For *in Him* (Jesus) we live and move and have our being" (Acts 17:28 NKJV, emphasis added). Sounds to me like we can't do very much without Him. He thinks so anyway.

I have an exercise I would like you to do as you continue reading. I suggest doing it physically, but you may do it mentally by picturing what I'm describing in your mind. I do it all the time to help me stay fresh and sensitive to what living my life from the inside out looks like. When I do this regularly, throughout the day, it makes me more sensitive to living my life like who I am in Christ—a new creation. Those with whom I've shared this have had the same testimony.

Stretch both of your arms outward with your palms facing away from you. The palms of your hands represent your soul—how you feel, the way you think, and what you do. Facing outward, your soul is getting its signals and information for how to do life from the world, a system that has been corrupted by sin.

Keeping your arms extended, slowly turn both palms toward yourself. This motion represents bringing to the inside the information you've gleaned from the world. This is how life is lived from the outside in. When your palms are facing away from you, the radar of your soul is picking up its signals from the external environment and bringing them to the inside. By doing this, your perceptions for how to live come from a contaminated source. This is a picture of what it looks like to live *in the flesh*—if you have not had a born-from-above experience with Christ. This is the only way the spiritually dead can live (1 Corinthians 1:18 NKJV). There are no other options. This is also what it looks like to live your life *by the flesh* if you have had a born-from-above experience. As a new creation in Christ, you are no longer *in the flesh* (Romans 8:9), but it is possible to *live by the flesh* (Romans 8:5).

Stretch out both of your arms again. With your arms stretched out, slowly turn both of your palms so they face you. Don't forget that your palms represent your soul—thinking, feeling, and doing. This inward position of your palms is to illustrate how you get and receive instruction for how to live your life with God as your Source. You're receiving information for how to live from the inside, the spirit realm, and then manifesting it on the outside. This is new creation living—living your life from the inside out. This is what walking in the spirit looks like. Our spirits receive instructions from God, and we live our lives accordingly. Outside in is living by the flesh; inside out is living by the spirit. We get to decide which way we live our lives.

Let's not abandon this exercise just yet. A person who has not had a born-from-above experience with the Lord Jesus Christ has only one option for living, and that is from the outside in. Since their spirits are dead, they do not have the ability to receive and perceive from the Spirit of God. The Spirit of God is the One who speaks to our spirits—not to our souls or bodies. Since individuals without Christ are spiritually dead, they have no way of receiving from God. They are spiritually unplugged. There is a disconnection (1 Corinthians 2:14).

A person without Christ is as *worse off* as they possibly can be. How worse off can a person be than the one who is separated from God for eternity? A highly respected, morally upright person who is not in union with Christ shares the same destiny as the morally despicable. Their eternal destinies are the same. Both will spend eternity separated from the presence of God. One may be worse than the other, but both are as *worse off* as they possibly can be.

Living by the Flesh

Let's define *flesh* before we proceed. The flesh is simply the soul living independently from God (thinking and feeling) and expressing this independence through the body (doing). This is precisely what I mean by "living from the outside in." It is getting our instructions for living from the external environment. This is the only source that is available for someone who has not become a new creation in Christ. Since this external source has been defiled by sin, it can only produce contaminated fruit—no matter how good it may appear:

> Now the works of the flesh are evident, which are: adultery, fornication, uncleanness, lewdness, idolatry, sorcery, hatred, contentions, jealousies, outbursts of wrath, selfish ambitions, dissensions, heresies, envy, murders, drunkenness, revelries, and the like; of which I tell you beforehand, just as I also told you in time past, that those who practice such things will not inherit the kingdom of God. (Galatians 5:19–21 NKJV)

This is not a pretty picture, is it? Living by the flesh never is.

Living by the Spirit

Even though we are new creation beings, it's still possible for us to think the way we did before we were made new creations. We have a choice now that we did not have when we were in the flesh—in our *unregenerate conditions*. We can choose how we live. We can live from the outside in, which is to allow the external environment to determine how we think and feel, or we can live from the inside out, which is to allow the internal presence of the Spirit of God to provide the instructions for how we are to live. How we think will determine how we behave. We can choose the way we think because thinking has now become a choice.

Extend both of your arms again. I know. Humor me. This time, while you have both arms extended, have one hand facing outward and one hand facing inward. Don't forget that our hands are representing our souls. The palm facing out is receiving communication from the external environment: the world's system. This soul is set on the flesh and lives by the flesh, which is the only thing that's possible for it to do. The palm facing inward is receiving its communication from the internal environment. This soul is set on the Spirit/spirit, empowering it to live by the Spirit.

What we have now is a divided soul. What is the outcome of this state of being? James gives us the answer in his short epistle. He says that a *double-minded* person (a two-soul person) will be unstable in everything they do (James 1:8 NLT). Then he says, "Such people should not expect to receive anything from the Lord" (James 1:7 NKJV). James used the term *double-minded* (Greek: *di psuchos*, two souls) again in chapter 4:8 (NKJV). This is the reason life is such a struggle for most Christians. We try to live successful, faith-based lives from the information we receive from our physical environments, and at the same time, we are trying to live our new creation lives. This is not something we do on purpose; we just don't know because we haven't been taught.

From the moment we enter this world as newborns, we begin the process of learning how to get our needs met from external sources. It doesn't take long for a baby to learn that crying will get them fed, attention, held, and rocked. This indoctrination of getting our needs met from this world's system continues as we grow and mature in our humanity. Then comes the moment when we say yes to God's invitation to life and become new creations in Christ. We know things are different now, but what we don't know is that we have taken our old way of thinking into our new creation living. Since we have learned how to manipulate people and our external environments to get our needs met—independent of God—this is our modus operandi for living our new creation lives. This is the reason why most Christians are working so hard at trying to become what they already are in Christ.

If we are going to be new creation thinkers, we must have a starting place. It begins with knowing how God sees us. He sees us as new creation beings because our old selves do not exist anymore (Romans 6:6 KJV). We will explore this in the next chapter.

CHAPTER 2

SEEING OURSELVES AS JESUS IS— NOT AS HE WAS

———

Are you a new creation? You are if you have had a born-from-above experience with the Lord Jesus Christ:

> Anyone who belongs to Christ has become a new person. *The old life is gone; a new life has begun.* (2 Corinthians 5:17 NLT, emphasis added)

Our old lives may be gone, but our old ways of thinking are still calling the shots. This is our problem. We have a greater affinity with our old selves than we do with our new selves. In Christ, we are new creations. Since we are new creations, we need to start thinking like who we really are.

The Good, the Bad, and the Ugly of Comparisons

Comparisons in and of themselves are not inherently bad. We live in a world of comparisons. Even though we are *not of the world*, we are certainly *in the world*. Comparisons are deep-rooted in our culture—from shopping, to which school we will send our kids, to comparing the food and service we get at different restaurants. Comparing prices for goods and services is not a bad thing. Who doesn't want to save money? Comparisons can go from being a positive thing to being a negative thing when we begin to compare ourselves with others. Comparing ourselves with others is not a good thing. Who wants to feel *less than*?

Comparisons have an upside and a downside. On the upside, comparisons can challenge us to rise up and become better at whatever we do. If you have a desire to learn how to be better at what you love doing, you will always look for those who can do it better. If you want to learn how to play golf better, you don't ask for instructions from someone who is worse at the game than you are. No. You look for people who can play better than you do. This is the natural and healthy way that comparisons can be positive and beneficial.

Comparisons also have a downside, especially if our self-worth and personal values come from comparing ourselves to other people. No matter how good or efficient we may be in a particular area, we will always find someone who can do it better. The fruit from such comparisons are feelings of inferiority, doubt, self-hatred, insecurity, depression, and the like. This is certainly not the fruit of the Spirit that Paul talks about in the book of Galatians.

Have you noticed that when we compare ourselves to others, we usually choose someone who we are fairly certain we will come out on the top end of the comparison? We may say things like, "I may not be living like I should, but at least I'm not as bad as so-and-so." We get a twisted sense of satisfaction from thinking that we are *better than* someone who we feel is *less than*. This gives birth to perverted feelings of superiority. We look down on those who we feel are not measuring up. This comparison game can become a narcotic, our drug of choice. We get a short-lived high from measuring ourselves to those who are not living up to our self-imposed standards.

Mark Twain said, "Comparison is the death of joy." Paul addressed the issue of comparing oneself to others in his second letter to the Corinthians. They had fallen victim to the enemy's comparison game. They were measuring themselves against others:

> Oh, don't worry; we wouldn't dare say that we are as wonderful as these other men who tell you how important they are! But *they are only comparing themselves with each other, using themselves as the standard of measurement.* How ignorant! (2 Corinthians 10:12 NLT, emphasis added)

Paul uses some very strong language in his rebuke of those in the church who had succumbed to the enemy's ploy of comparing people by people: "How ignorant!" When we use people as our standard for measuring our own self-worth, we are just as ignorant.

The Enemy Will See You the Same Way That You See Yourself

Years ago, I was reading the story about Moses sending spies into the land of Canaan to scout it out when I saw something that rocked my world. The following two sentences sum up what the Holy Spirit revealed to me that day:

> The enemy will always acknowledge you the same way you acknowledge yourself. He will see us the way we see ourselves. (Numbers 13:33 NKJV)

I encourage you to read those two sentences one more time because this is the foundational premise for this book.

After spying out the land for forty days, the CIA (Canaan Information Agency) returned to give their report to Moses, Aaron, and the congregation of the children of Israel who were camped in the wilderness. Here is their assessment of the land God promised them:

> There we saw the giants (the descendants of Anak came from the giants); and *we were like grasshoppers in our own sight, and so we were in their sight.* (Numbers 13:33 NKJV, emphasis added).

Pay close attention to the report they gave, especially to the syntax of their statement. When they saw the giants who were living in the land of Canaan, they were consumed by fear. They were overwhelmed by anxiety because they were comparing themselves to the inhabitants of the land. The people of God saw themselves as nothing more than insects (grasshoppers), and that is exactly how their enemy saw them. One translation renders the last part of this verse in this way:

> *Next to them* (comparison) *we felt like grasshoppers,* and *that's what they thought, too.* (Numbers 13:33 NLT, emphasis added).

Millions of people did not get to enjoy God's Promised Land because of this one comparison. The land that was promised to them would be enjoyed by their descendants. I wonder how many promises we may have forfeited by getting trapped in the enemy's comparison snare, distracting us so we do not see ourselves as new creations in Christ.

I have shared my testimony hundreds of times about how the Lord used 1 John 4:17 to radically transform my understanding about the new person I have become because I am now in Christ. Once the Holy Spirit embeds the truth of this verse in the depths of your innermost being, it will radically alter your life for the better—forever:

> Love has been perfected among us in this: that we
> may have boldness in the day of judgment; because
> *as He is, so are we in this world.* (1 John 4:17 NKJV,
> emphasis added)

The last nine words in this verse got ahold of me that day. The truth of it has gotten stronger over time, and it is bringing more revelation concerning a Christian's true identity. "As He is, so are we in this world." We are like Him now? That's what this verse says. If you have doubts, read this verse again—and again if you have to. There is something even more eye-opening in this verse that's easily missed. It says our identities come from "Who He is" and not Who He was. I told you it is a game changer.

Like the majority of believers, I was a strong advocate for distance-and-delay theology. This was not something I was conscious of, and I do not believe others are either. Because we are so connected to our physical environments, we are convinced that most of our new creation birthright privileges are laid up for us in heaven (distance), and we will get to enjoy them someday (delay). Until then, we will have to do all we can, the best we can, to enjoy what God has procured for us through His Son, Jesus Christ. This is especially true when it comes to our spiritual identities. We even have scripture to support our distance-and-delay position:

> Beloved, now we are children of God; and it has not
> yet been revealed what we shall be, but *we know* that
> when He is revealed, *we shall be like Him*, for we shall
> see Him as He is. (1 John 3:2 NKJV, emphasis added)

Sometimes it is helpful to see what a scripture does not say in order to see what it really says. In this verse, our attention is drawn to these words: "It has not yet been revealed what we shall be." We miss the "but we know" part of the verse. What will we know when Jesus returns? We shall be like Him. This verse doesn't say that we will become like Jesus. You can't become what Christ has already made you to be. We are like Him now in our new creation life. "As He is so are we in this world" (1 John 4:17).

When will we be like Jesus? We are like Him now. This was the exchange that was made when we accepted and received Jesus Christ's invitation to new lives. In our spirit lives, we were made what He was because He was willing to be made what we were. Let me state it another way: Jesus was made what we were so we could be what He is (2 Corinthians 5:21 NKJV).

New Creation Identity

Most Christians are quick to point out that they adhere to the infallibility of the scriptures: The Word of God is divinely inspired and without error (2 Timothy 3:16). And they do—until it goes against their experiences. There is a well-known scripture that most Christians can recite verbatim. If they can't quote it word for word, they can at least give you the spirit of it:

> Therefore, if anyone is in Christ (you are, aren't you),
> he is a new creation; *old things have passed away*;
> behold, *all things have become new.* (2 Corinthians
> 5:17 NKJV), emphasis added)

If we are new creations in Christ, shouldn't we be thinking like what we have become? But this will never happen if we don't see ourselves in the way God sees us. Our old way of thinking does not adapt itself to our new creation identities because it cannot. We need to start seeing ourselves in the way God sees us, but we can't do that until we know how He sees us.

Our focus has been on the wrong thing for a long time. More concentration has been given to our humanity when the center of our attention should be on His divinity. This is what Paul is addressing in his second letter to the church in Corinth:

> Therefore, from now on, *we regard no one according to flesh*. Even though *we have known Christ according to the flesh*, yet now we know Him thus no longer. (2 Corinthians 5:16 NKJV, emphasis added)

Pay close attention to what Paul says in this verse. There was a time when we knew Jesus in His humanity (flesh), but that is no longer the case. In the very next verse, he writes, "Therefore, *if anyone is in Christ*, he is a new creation" (2 Corinthians 5:17 NKJV). Jesus is called Christ, which reveals his true nature. Jesus is His human side, and Christ is His divine side. This is what the incarnation was all about. Christ's divinity lived in Jesus's humanity.

In Paul's first letter to the church in Corinth, he said, "Or do you not know that your body (human side) is the temple of the Holy Spirit (divine side) (1 Corinthians 6:19 NKJV, emphasis added). That is exactly what transpired when you accepted and received Jesus Christ as your Lord and Savior: divinity inhabited humanity. Your flesh is your human side, and Christ in you is your divine side. Your spiritual identity does not come from your humanity; your identity comes from Christ's divinity. Let me state it another way. Your humanity came from your physical birth— when you were born from below. Your spiritual identity comes from your spiritual birth—when you were born from above. Our new creation identities come from who Jesus is and not from who He was. "As He is, so are we in this world" (1 John 4:17 NKJV). To know Him after the flesh is to know Him as He was. To know Him in the Spirit is to know Him as He is. Again, our identities come from who He is.

Let's continue to think our way through identifying with Jesus as He is and not as He was. Paul wrote the following words from a Philippian jail cell:

> Let this mind be in you which was also in Christ (divine) Jesus (human), who, being in the form of God, did not consider it robbery to be equal with God, but made Himself of no reputation, *taking the form of a bondservant, and coming in the likeness of men.* And being found *in the appearance as a man,* He humbled Himself and became obedient to the point of death, even the death of the cross. (Philippians 2:5–8 NKJV, emphasis added)

Jesus put on an earth suit and came into this world. He related to us in His humanity to make it possible for us relate to Him in His divinity. I'm going to say it one more time because this is the key to understanding our new creation identities: Jesus's humanity is Who He was. His divinity is Who He is. This is the very reason Paul said that we no longer know Jesus as he was—in His humanity (2 Corinthians 5:16 NKJV).

So many of us find it difficult to live up to our callings as children of God because we have had the wrong focus. Our attention has been riveted on Jesus's humanity when it should be on His divinity. This is something the majority of the family of faith has not been taught. We should not blame our mentors if they did not teach us about the significance of our new creation identities that we have in Christ. You can't give what you don't know you have.

Seeing Ourselves as God Sees Us

God sees us through the eyes of His divinity. He sees us as new creations. Since He made us new, He sees us as He made us. This is the only way He can see us. We may have a difficult time seeing ourselves the way He does because our experiences don't always measure up to our new identities. How does God see you? This is what matters. Once we start seeing ourselves the way our Creator sees us now, we start thinking as new creations—inside out. When God looks at you, He says the same thing He said in Genesis 1 and 2 when He created the world and all that is in it: "It is good" (Genesis 1:31 NKJV).

Let me give you a simple illustration with the hope it will help you understand your new creation identity better. Hopefully, it will help you see yourself as Jesus is—not as He was. Picture a solid gold coin in your hand. Inscribed on the coin is the name Jesus. Jesus is called the *last Adam* and the *second Man* in 1 Corinthians 15:45–48. The name Jesus speaks to His humanity, and His name was given to Him by God. The angel Gabriel was given an assignment by God to tell Mary that she had been handpicked to give birth to His Son. "And behold, you will conceive in your womb and bring forth a Son, and *shall call His name Jesus*" (Luke 1:31 NKJV, emphasis added). God literally wrapped Himself up in human flesh and birthed Himself. Mary gave birth to the Child Jesus, giving Him His human side (Isaiah 9:6 NKJV). God sent His Son to live in Jesus, giving Him His divine side (Isaiah 9:6; Galatians 4:4 NKJV). This is why He is called Jesus (humanity) Christ (divinity). This is the incarnation, beloved.

Let's say that one day while fondling the coin in your hand, you inadvertently flipped it over. To your utter amazement, another name appears. It is the name Christ. Even though it's still the same coin, the name is different. It is one coin, but it has two sides. The Jesus side represents His humanity (who He was), and the Christ side represents His divinity (who He is). Since we have been gifted with free will, we have the freedom to choose which side gets our undivided attention: who Jesus was or who Jesus is. Hopefully, you are beginning to get a little insight into your new creation identity. Your *old life* identified with who Jesus was. Your *new life* identifies with Who Jesus is. Keep the last nine words of 1 John 4:17 in mind as you process this incredible truth: *"as He is, so are we* in this world." I'm going to hit this nail on the head as many times as needed to drive home the truth of our new creation identities. If you have had a born-from-above experience, the new you is as He is—not as He was.

How do we fit in this illustration? I'm glad you asked. Let's pretend you have another coin in your hand, and it also has two sides. Once again, the only difference are the names on the coin. On one side are the words "my old life." On the other side are the words "my new life." Instead of the words *old life* and *new life,* we could use the biblical terms *natural* and *spiritual* (1 Corinthians 2:14–16 NKJV). We could also use the words *lost* and *saved,* which most people in the community of faith are more familiar with. Be honest with yourself. Where is your focus? Is it on the humanity side (the *old* you) or the divinity side (the *new* you)? You have a choice. The old you is who you were before you had your Christ encounter. The new you is who you are now (after your encounter with Christ).

One side of the coin represents the flesh (the human self), and the other side reveals our new creation identities (our spiritual selves). The side we set our focus on will determine how we think, feel, and act. A person's behavior will mimic what they believe. Our sights will be on the flesh or on the spirit. The choice is ours. How you see yourself will be determined by which side of the coin you are giving the most attention to.

Jesus chose to identify with us in His humanity so we could have the opportunity to identify with Him in His divinity (2 Corinthians 5:21 NKJV). Here's some good news. If you are a part of God's forever family, He sees you as the new creation He made *you to be* not *as you were.* God wants us to see ourselves the same way He sees us. It's time we begin. Normal Christianity focuses more on behavior than belief, which causes a person to work hard to become what Christ has already made them to be. I'll say again what I said in the preface of this book: it will take faith and a whole lot of courage to walk away from normal Christianity.

So many believers struggle with their eternal security and self-worth and the fear that they are not loved by God because they still see themselves as their old human selves, which the Word of God calls *the flesh*. Paul talks about this extensively in Romans 7. If we set our minds *on the flesh*, we will find ourselves living *by the flesh*. There is a huge difference between setting one's mind on the flesh and being in the flesh:

> But *you are not in the flesh* but in the Spirit, if indeed the Spirit of God dwells in you. Now if anyone does not have the Spirit of Christ, he is not His. (Romans 8:9 NKJV, emphasis added)

The new you can no more reenter the flesh any more than the old you could enter the spirit. God will not cohabit with sin. The old you was crucified with Christ (Romans 6:6 NKJV). When Christ was raised from the dead, the new you was raised with Him (Romans 6:1–14 NKJV). Your new creation identity comes for the resurrected Christ: "As He is, so are you in this world" (1 John 4:17 NKJV).

We need to start seeing ourselves the way Christ sees us. Believe me when I say that it will antagonize religious spirits when we do. If religious spirits are intrinsically hostile, why not throw more fuel on the fire by knowing and openly declaring your new creation identity. Since we will be engaged in spiritual warfare as long as we are in this world, let's fight the good fight of faith (1 Timothy 6:12 NKJV). We may lose a few battles, sustain some injuries, and look foolish at times, but praise the Lord because the war has already been won. Christ won—so we win too!

Christ sees us as new creations (2 Corinthians 4:17 NKJV). He sees us as being holy, righteous, complete, sinless, loved unconditionally, and so much more. Here's the eye-opener: Christ wants us to see ourselves through His eyes. Since we bear His divine nature, this is possible—as long as we are focused on the right side of the coin (2 Peter 1:4 NKJV).

God took up residence in the new us, to live through us, as us. Our spirit lives are expressed through our souls when we live from the inside out: what we think, how we feel, and the way we act. This is what salvation is all about.

One of the greatest passages on who we are as new creation beings is found in Paul's second letter to the church in Corinth. Soak in these four verses until they begin to leach into your spirit:

> Either way, Christ's love controls us. Since we believe that Christ died for all, we also believe that *we have all died to our old life*. He died for everyone so that those *who receive his new life* will no longer live for themselves. Instead, they will live for Christ, who died and was raised for them. So we have stopped evaluating others from a human point of view. At one time we thought of Christ merely from a human point of view. *How differently we know him now*! This means that anyone who belongs to Christ *has become a new person*. *The old life* is gone; a *new life* has begun. (2 Corinthians 5:14–17 NLT, emphasis added)

If the reality of this truth ever gets into the core of your innermost being, you will never be the same. The moment you said yes to the Lord's invitation to life, you received His new life; you became a brand-new person. Your old life is gone, and your new life has begun. Old-life thinking is not designed for new life living. It is high time we start thinking like the new creations we have become in Christ.

If we have been Christians for a while and been actively involved in church life for a period of time, it's possible to be able to quote scripture with the best of them. However, we need to keep in mind that quoting scripture is not the same as being spiritually mature. You can talk about something and not know it, but you can't know something and not talk about it. If we truly know Jesus—not just knowing about Jesus—we will not be able to restrain ourselves from bragging about Him.

If what you believe about God—the way He sees you, what He thinks about you, and how he feels about you—does not produce the fruit of peace and rest, then what you believe is wrong.

CHAPTER 3

BEING SO EARTHLY MINDED THAT WE ARE OF NO HEAVENLY GOOD

———

Oliver Wendell Homes said, "Some people are so heavenly minded that they are of no earthly good." This exposes the biggest struggle that Christians are engaged in, and it reveals the answer to overcoming this struggle. This is a catchy turn of phrase for sure, but is it true?

Given the present spiritual condition of the average local church today, we could use more heavenly thinkers in our ranks. This may create some concerns for those in leadership positions and for those who have become comfortable with their religious rituals, but I don't think new creation thinkers should be on our list of worries. There are bigger fish to fry—like taking the good news of the Gospel of Jesus Christ to our world before it's eternally too late.

Most believers have become so worldly minded that heavenly thinking makes them uncomfortable. New creation thinking is considered by them to be borderline crazy—if not full-blown heresy. You might hear this retort from earthly thinking Christians when they hear new creation thinking expressed: "Who do they think they are? So-and-so has become a religious fanatic." One of our major problems as believers is that we don't know who we are in Christ.

When you first read the title of this chapter, you may have thought I misrepresented what Mr. Holmes is accredited to have said. Well, you read it right the first time. I tweaked it a little because if it were left untweaked, it would not be true when it comes to new creation thinking.

The Word of God says, "For in Him we live and move and have our being" (Acts 17:28 NKJV). If this is true—and I contend that it is—then our thinking should be more heavenly than earthly. I'm convinced that most Christians are not making more of a heavenly impact on their communities because they are too earthly minded.

As new creations in Christ, we should be so heavenly minded that we are of earthly good. When we begin to think and talk like who we are in Christ, we begin to make a huge difference in our world—for the better.

Earthly Thinking Is Our Problem

I had some pretty good talks with my mother after I surrendered my life to preach the Gospel. I may not have known very much, but I was running over with excitement. She could tell by my exuberance and unending chatter that I was serious. Everything in our conversation was copacetic until she felt I was taking my relationship with the Lord too far. I was so on fire for Jesus that I couldn't help but talk about Him and what He had done for me.

When I told her I was surrendering my life to preach, she said, "I sure hope you're not doing this to get out of work."

Those words grieved my spirit, but I never let on how they made me feel. She perceived our conversation as getting out of the realm of normal Christian thinking, and she said, "You know, son, we can be so heavenly minded that we are of no earthly good." Since I certainly did not want to be weird or be considered a religious extremist, I retreated from our conversation.

Fifty years later, I'm still on fire for the Lord. I would say that I love Him more now than I did then. I also understand why people quote Mr. Homes when they feel things are getting too personal or if conversations about new creation identity begin to make them uncomfortable. It's okay to talk about Jesus on Sunday because that is what Sundays are for, but let's not take this thing too far by having serious conversations about our new creation identities during the week. We certainly do not want to expose ourselves to a spirituality that is outside of our comfort zones. That could cause us to be of no earthly good.

What my mother said to me the day I told her that I had given my life to preaching the Gospel was not out of meanness, and it was not designed to get me back in line with normal Christianity. Like most Christians, she didn't know what to say. The news of full-bore commitment to the things of God frightens most people. My mother was not comfortable with any discussion that was outside of normal Christianity. To her credit, she did become a staunch supporter of me and my ministry for many years before she was promoted to heaven. She was my best PR person for many years. In her later years, we had some incredible in-depth talks about new creation identity, believer's birthright privileges, and so much more. She began to step out of normal Christianity, and she never knew it. The peace and freedom that it brought to her overshadowed everything else. My mother is in heaven now, and she knows firsthand what I'm still trying to discover. If I could hear her speak, here's what I think she would be saying: "Son, don't be so earthly minded that you are of no heavenly good." She would get a rousing amen from me.

If earthly mindedness is the Achilles' heel for most believers, then what does it look like? It is simply getting our living instructions and the majority of our information from the world's system—to the exclusion of the Word of God. Society and culture determine our lifestyles. Worldly thinking is working hard to get all you can, can all you get, and then sit on the can. It is focused on getting. Heavenly mindedness is consumed with giving. This is when we are of earthly good. Being earthly minded is seeing God as only an add-on: He is an attachment to the way we live our lives. We certainly do not want to get too serious about our faith because it could interfere with our having a good time. Earthly mindedness is living our lives from the outside in. I would suggest that you go back and read chapter 1 again—more slowly this time.

Heavenly Thinking Is the Solution to Our Problem

The Word of God never warns us not to be too heavenly minded. I don't remember Jesus ever having to rebuke His disciples for having too much faith or scolding them for being too heavenly minded. When we become more heavenly focused, the more we will impact our world for the better:

> Since you have been raised to new life with Christ, *set your sights on the realities of heaven*, where Christ sits in the place of honor at God's right hand. *Think about the things of heaven*, not the things of earth. For you died to this life, and *your real life is hidden with Christ in God*. And when *Christ, who is your life*, is revealed to the whole world, you will share in all his glory. (Colossians 3:1–4 NLT, emphasis added)

This scripture completely reverses the declaration of the parable we began this chapter with. If we are going to live victorious lives while we are in this earthly realm, we must always remember that the word of man goes nowhere when it is in contradiction to the Word of God.

Paul's instructions to the Colossians were not just for them; they are for all believers. We are to set our sights (our minds, our thoughts) on the realities of heaven. It sounds to me like God wants all of His children to be more heavenly minded so we can be of earthly good. Allow this truth to get past your natural thought processes and let it sink deep inside your innermost being. Once it is embedded in your spirit and takes root, you will never be the same.

Setting our thoughts on the realities of heaven is a choice. It will have to be done on purpose. Living in spiritual reality while living in this natural realm must be intentional. No one will force you—and it will not be easy—because it goes against what the world's system has taught us. We have allowed the world to conform us to its way of thinking even though God has warned us not to allow this to happen:

> Don't copy the behavior and customs of this world, but *let God transform you into a new person by changing the way you think.* Then you will learn to know God's will for you, which is good and pleasing and perfect. (Romans 12:2 NLT, emphasis added)

Our minds must be transformed by the Spirit of God.

Our old selves died when Christ died and was buried. When Christ was raised from the dead, our new selves were raised with Him. What sustained our old lives cannot sustain the new lives that we have in Christ. The biggest struggles of Christians come from trying to incorporate their old ways of thinking in their new creation minds. Since we have been born from above, we need to set our minds on things above (Colossians 3:2 NKJV). We need to start thinking like the new creations we are in Christ. This takes faith and courage because it is out of the realm of normal Christianity. The chances are good that other believers will see you as being strange. They may think you have lost your mind—and they are right! You now have the mind of Christ (1 Corinthians 2:16 NKJV).

The writer of the book of Hebrews tells us that we are to live by faith and not by facts. It's not that we deny facts, but we have chosen to confess truth. The Word of God is truth (John 17:17 NKJV). The writer of Hebrews goes on to say that it's impossible to please God without faith (Hebrews 11:6 NKJV). We don't need sight to support our faith:

> Faith is the confidence that what we hope for will actually happen; *it* (faith) *gives us assurance about things we cannot see.* (Hebrews 11:1 NLT, emphasis added)

Go back and read this verse again—slowly this time. Is it really possible to believe something is true even though we can't see it? We can when we set our minds on things above. When our minds are set on things below, it is a different story. To tell someone you are believing in something that you can't see would be considered insane. If you can see it, it's not faith.

New Creation Thinking Can Make You Look Foolish

For the past six years, my precious wife has been fighting cancer. There have been some highs and some very low moments during this process, but not one time have I heard my beloved complain. I have never seen anyone more courageous than she is.

The prognosis we were given was not one of hope. After the oncologist gave their report, it felt like the air in the room had been sucked out, which was followed by a long period of silence. After we processed the information that was given to us, we made our decision. We would never repeat what we were told by the medical team that day. Our decision was to move forward, confessing the truth, and not allow facts to rob us of our confidence or steal our hope.

We understand that the only thing doctors have at their disposal are facts. We are not denying the facts of their report, but we have chosen to confess the truth that is found in the scriptures because truth trumps facts every time. The truth is, "By His stripes we are healed" (Isaiah 53:5 NKJV; 1 Peter 2:24 NKJV).

I will never forget the look on the doctor's face when I said, "We hear what you are saying, but this report will never be repeated by us. What we have been told today will never come out of our mouths. This will not be our confession." I went on to say, "I can't wait for the day when you pronounce that my wife is free of cancer." All I could see on the doctor's face was a no-vacancy-sign stare. They could not wrap their mind around what I had said. I could read their thoughts like a cheap novel: *Bless their hearts—they are in a state of shock and are denying reality.* The doctor immediately began to give us information about the counseling services that were at our disposal.

I know you might be thinking, *What if?* I know exactly what you are about to say. Haven't you prayed for someone's healing—and then they died? Sure, I have. Here's what I did. I prayed for the next one. And I'll pray for the next one. Believing God for what appears to be impossible is new creation thinking, and it can make you look like you have lost your mind. It is outside the realm of normal Christianity. There will be times when you will be perceived as one who's lost touch with reality. Maybe you have. It all depends on which reality you are talking about. When you set your sights on the realities of heaven, you will never lose. A child of God will receive healing on this side of eternity—or they will step into eternity healed. Either way, it's a win-win situation. I'm not sure if we really understand what faith is. Faith is not about everything turning out all right. Faith is about being all right no matter how things turn out.

To date, my wife has had 109 chemo treatments and twenty radiation treatments. After her seventh treatment, my wife's oncologist asked me what I did for a living. Deep inside my *knower,* I knew that day would come. I had never heard anyone stutter and stammer like this doctor did when I told them I was a pastor. I have to admit that I loved it.

Believing for what you can't see is new creation thinking:

> Now faith is the substance of things hoped for, *the evidence of things not seen*. (Hebrews 11:1 NKJV, emphasis added)

If you can see it, then there is no need to expend faith. Faith is the currency given to us by God so we can purchase what He has made available to us in the spiritual realm:

> For in it (the Gospel) the righteousness of God is revealed from faith to faith; as it is written, "*The just shall live by faith*." (Romans 1:17 NKJV, emphasis added)

Seeing Earth through Heaven's Eyes

Pay close attention to what the Lord said in His prayer in John 17. What He says to His Father reveals how He sees earth through heaven's eyes:

> I have given them (us included) your word. And the world hates them because *they do not belong to the world*, just as I do not belong to the world. *I'm not asking you to take them out of the world*, but to keep them safe from the evil one. *They do not belong to this world any more than I do*. (John 17:14–17 NLT, emphasis added)

Jesus did not say that we are not *in this world*. He said we are not *of this world* any more than He is. If you are a new creation in Christ, you are still *in* this earthly realm. This fact cannot be denied. However, you are not *of* this earthly realm. If we never grasp this truth, we will spend our entire lives living like normal Christians. We will look at heavenly things through earthly eyes. We need to be seeing earth through heaven's eyes.

Why have we become so comfortable with thinking like the world does? The answer is simple. We are convinced that our physical environments are more real than our spiritual environments. We allow facts to control how we feel, what we think, and how we see things. Truth should be the thermostat that controls how we live. As long as we are on this side of eternity, we need to think like who we are in Christ. When we are thinking and acting like who Christ has made us to be, we are bringing the unseen realm into the seen realm. This is how people get to see the unseen God. They see Him in you and in me. This is what it means to be so heavenly minded that we are of some earthly good.

Our strong world mentalities keep us from enjoying our spiritual realities. For the majority of those within the community of faith, normal Christianity is hunky-dory. Whatever you do, don't mess with their comfort zones. Anything out of the norm is viewed as strange and weird. They may not say it, but they sure think it: *We need to stay away from "those people" because they have taken their faith way too far.* I really like what Smith Wigglesworth said: "You can't go too far with Christ. As a matter of fact, you can't go far enough." It's easy to say amen to this declaration, but living it is another thing.

Capture Your Thoughts

There is one thing we must get a handle on. If God tells you to do something, it's possible for you to do it. This sounds logical to most of us, but I can't tell you how many times I've heard people say, "I can't forgive that person," "I can't control my temper," or "I can't help the way I feel about that individual." The *I can't* list is endless. You actually can do what God tells you to do. You just don't want to. If we blame the impossible for not doing the possible, we find a little relief in our conscience. I would obey, but what I'm being told to do is impossible. It's not about *can* do; it's about *will* do:

> Casting down arguments and every high thing that
> exalts itself against the knowledge of God; *bringing*
> *every thought into captivity* to the obedience of
> Christ. (2 Corinthians 10:5 NKJV, emphasis added)

We are instructed by the Word of God to take control of our thought lives. How does one do that? It will certainly not be something that happens automatically. It has to be intentional. We all have those come-to-Jesus moments when we realize we have spent too much time mulling over unhealthy thoughts that are antagonistic to our new creation identity. When this happens, don't condemn yourself. Don't quit. It will take time and a whole lot of practice. You may find a little relief in knowing you will never attain 100 percent accuracy in taking your thoughts captive while you are in this world, but you should not let that deter you from starting.

You cannot control thoughts from invading the space between your ears, but you have maximum control of how long they squat there. There is a quote by Martin Luther that is apropos: "You cannot keep birds from flying over your head, but you can keep them from building a nest in your hair." This is true when it is applied to our thought lives. The enemy will do his best to infiltrate our minds with inappropriate thoughts, but we have the authority to not let them live rent-free in our heads. We don't have to act on them. When we practice capturing our thoughts, we become more sensitive to the thoughts that filter through our minds. We also become more skilled at taking them captive.

Choose What You Think About

> And now, dear brothers and sisters one final thing.
> *Fix your thoughts* on what is true, and honorable,
> and right, and pure, and lovely, and admirable.

> *Think about things* that are excellent and worthy of
> praise. (Philippians 4:8 NLT, emphasis added)

Paul must have been a Baptist preacher. When he said, "One final thing," he did not mean a thing. He may be buzzing the airport, but he may not be ready to land the plane yet.

> Fix your thoughts on what is true; think about
> things that are excellent.

God will not tell us to do something that is impossible for us to do. Healthy thinking must be done on purpose. When the enemy tries to infiltrate your thought life with unhealthy suggestions, stop immediately and begin to think about what is true, what is honorable, what is right and pure, and what is lovely and admirable. You will be amazed at how much more control you will have in determining what comes into your head and how long it stays there. The more you practice this, the more you will impact your world for the better.

> *Guard your heart* above all else, for *it determines the*
> *course of your life.* (Proverbs 4:23 NLT, emphasis
> added)

The responsibility for guarding our hearts (thoughts) was given to us by our Creator. We are blessed with free will, which gives us the ability to take all our thoughts captive. This is very important because our thoughts determine the direction of our lives:

> Today I have *given you the choice* between life and
> death, between blessings and curses. Now I call on
> heaven and earth to witness *the choice you make.*
> Oh, that you would *choose life*, so that you and your
> descendants might live. (Deuteronomy 30:19 NLT,
> emphasis added)

Circumstances do not determine the quality of life we enjoy—our choices do:

> Don't copy the behavior and customs of this world, but let God transform you into a new person *by changing the way you think.* (Romans 12:2 NLT, emphasis added)

When we exchanged our old lives for new ones, we became new creations. We now have the ability to think differently. The old patterns of thinking will not work in our new lives. The old system has been unplugged. It cannot supply power to who Christ has made us to be. Changing the way we think will radically change our perspectives, which will change how we live our lives. The struggles that Christians find themselves in come from trying to live their new lives with their old ways of thinking.

Dr. Caroline Leaf said, "When you think, you build thoughts, and these become physical substances in your brain." She also said, "As we think, we change the physical nature of our brain. As we consciously direct our thinking, we can wire out toxic patterns of thinking and replace them with healthy thoughts." Wow!

Jesus gave Himself for you, so He could give Himself to you, so He can live His life through you—as you. There is only one requirement for this to be a reality: You must die to yourself, and there is nothing as strong as self-preservation.

CHAPTER 4

AS NEW CREATIONS, WE HAVE THE MIND OF CHRIST

It is possible to tell the truth without actually telling the truth. If you don't believe that, then the next time a politician says something—anything—listen intently. They can tell a lie by telling the truth. This skill is called paltering. Paltering is simply manipulating the truth to give credibility to a lie. No one is more skilled at paltering than our elected officials.

Paltering is a common negotiation tactic. Let me give you an example. Pretend you are giving a potential buyer a tour of the facility you have for sale.

This potential buyer is asking you a plethora of questions as you show them the building. "Does the roof leak?" asks the potential buyer.

"We put a new roof on fifteen years ago," you respond.

It is true you had a new roof installed fifteen years ago, but this is not the question you were asked. You were asked if the roof leaked. To keep from telling a lie, you tell the truth. You did install a new roof, but there are spots where it leaks. You told the truth without actually telling the truth.

Most Christians would say they are against lying in any shape or form, and I believe they are. However, most of us lie in varying ways every day. "Not me," you say. Think about this the next time your wife asks if it looks like she has gained weight, and you respond, "Sweetheart, when you walked down the aisle on our wedding day thirty years ago, I felt like I had won the lottery." You told the truth, but you paltered. It is true your wife was a beautiful bride. When the music shifted gears, and she made her grand entrance, you almost lost your breath. You were so taken away by her beauty that you whispered to your best man, "I feel like I'm the richest man in the world." You did feel like the most blessed man on the planet. You told your wife the truth—but you didn't answer the question your wife asked you. There is no way you are going to tell her that it looks like she has gained sixty pounds. I could fill this book with illustrations about lies being told by telling the truth. Most of the time, we are not even conscious of what we are doing.

Christians are very good at paltering. I am convinced that most of us are not even aware of it. It is not uncommon to greet someone at church by saying, "How are you doing today?"

They respond, "You know, my life has not been the same since I accepted Christ as my Lord and Savior."

That is not what you asked them. You asked, "How are you doing *today.*" They have no idea that you saw them arguing with their spouse (quite loudly too) as they walked down the sidewalk toward the front door of the church. Instead of telling a lie, they told the truth. Their life has not been the same since they accepted and received Jesus as their Lord and Savior. By telling the truth, they actually told a lie.

Since we have the mind of Christ as new creations, we have the capability to think differently than we were able to before we had our born-from-above experience (1 Corinthians 2:16 NKJV). By not knowing our new creation identities, we don't know what we have in Christ. If the Word of God is true—it says that we have the mind of Christ—shouldn't we be able to do now what we were unable to do before and think differently.

Our Spiritual Condition before Christ

To understand who we are as children of God, it is important to be reminded of who we were before we were a part of God's forever family. I can't think of a better passage of scripture to help us with this than Ephesians 2:

> *Don't forget* that you Gentiles *used to be outsiders.* You were called "uncircumcised heathens" by the Jews, who were proud of their circumcision, even though it affected only their bodies and not their hearts. In those days *you were living apart from Christ. You were excluded* from citizenship among the people of Israel, and *you did not know* the covenant promises God had made to them. You lived in this world *without God* and *without hope.* (Ephesians 2:11–12 NLT, emphasis added)

I cannot imagine a more destitute picture of someone without God. This was our story before we were saved. If you are not saved, this is your story now. It's not a good one. You will not enjoy the ending.

The first words Paul says in this passage of scripture are, "Don't forget." Most translations use "remember." One renders it "keep in mind." Why would Paul begin with these words? Because it is so easy for us to forget what our spiritual condition was before we had our encounter with Christ. It was not a pretty one. If we forget who we were before Christ redeemed us, we might not appreciate—as we should—who we are since He repurchased us.

You may be thinking, *I thought the scriptures tell us not to live in the past* (Philippians 3:13–14 NKJV). That is not what Paul is saying when he tells us not to forget. God does not want His children *to live in the past*. He is simply saying, "If you really want to know who you are in Christ, then don't forget who you were before Christ." It is beneficial for us to remember what our spiritual condition was before we were made a part of God's forever family. Once again, remembering the past is not the same as living in the past.

I think most people are familiar with the quote accredited to George Santayana: "Those who cannot remember the past are condemned to repeat it." This is a truth you can take to the bank. Forgetting history can be very costly. I want to capture the spirit of this quote by Santayana by saying it in a way that I hope will help us understand who we used to be so we will be more thankful knowing who we are: If we forget what our spiritual condition was before we were believers, the chances are good that we will be deceived into believing that we can live our new creation lives with old creation thinking. This is not going to happen. Old creation thinking does not jibe with our new creation identities. This will not happen because it cannot happen.

In this Ephesian passage, Paul graphically describes our pre-Jesus lives. We were in serious trouble. He says three things about our spiritual conditions that I want to focus on: We were without Christ. We were without hope. We were without God.

Our Pre-Jesus Lives

We were without Christ. "At that time, *you were without Christ*" (Ephesians 2:12 NKJV, emphasis added). Mull over the last four words of this verse. What does it mean to be without Christ? Maybe Acts 17 can help us better understand: "For in Him (in Christ) we live and move and have our being" (Acts 17:28 NKJV). Allow me to paraphrase this verse. In Christ—and Christ alone—we live and move and have our existence.

Let's use this verse to define our pre-Jesus lives. Since we were not in Christ, we did not have life. This does not make sense to the natural mind. When we were born from below (physical birth), we received our natural lives. Acts 17 is not talking about natural life. It is talking about spiritual life. To be spiritually alive, you must have a second birthday. You may be more familiar with this expression: You must be born again.

Pay close attention to the wording of this verse. Those who consider the cross as being foolish are perishing now. It doesn't say they will perish someday. It says they are perishing at this very moment. They have physical life, but they are spiritually dead. This is why Jesus said to Nicodemus, "You must be born from above" (John 3:3 NKJV). You must have a second birthday to be spiritually alive.

Because we were without Christ in our pre-Jesus days, we were without hope. Life is found in Christ alone—and hope is too. Without Him, we have no hope. When a person has no hope, it's not *if* they will give up; it's a matter of *when* they will give up. Howard Hendricks gave an incredible definition of discouragement: "Discouragement is the anesthetic the devil uses on a person just before he reaches in and carves out his heart."

Pastor Ray Johnston piggybacks on this idea:

> When people lose hope, they lose their ability to dream for the future. Despair replaces joy. Fear replaces faith. Anxiety replaces prayer. Insecurity replaces confidence. Tomorrow's dreams are replaced by nightmares. It's a lousy way to live.

When you try to encourage a person who has reached the depths of despair by telling them there is always a light at the end of the tunnel, they perceive the light as an oncoming train.

"*Hope deferred* makes the heart sick" (Proverbs 13:12 NKJV, emphasis added). Hope is confident expectation. When hope is deferred confident expectation is placed on hold. An Italian proverb says, "Hope is the last thing ever lost"

In our pre-Jesus lives, we were without Christ, we were without hope, and we lived in this world without God. I find it interesting that Paul says we were without Christ and without God. Over the years, I've heard people say, "I believe in God, but I'm not sure about Jesus." These people are convinced they are spiritually okay because they believe in God, and they think this makes them Christians—but it doesn't. It makes them Deists.

Heaven is not a prepared place for Deists. Jesus said, "Let not your heart be troubled; you believe in God, *believe also in Me*" (John 14:1 NKJV). Jesus was God wrapped up in human flesh. If you accept God but reject Jesus, you are actually rejecting God. When you accept Jesus, you are also accepting God. There is no passage any clearer on this truth than the one found in 1 John:

> Who is a liar but he who denies that *Jesus is the Christ*? He is *antichrist who denies the Father and the Son*. Whoever denies the Son (Jesus) does not have the Father (God) either; he who acknowledges the Son (Jesus) has the Father (God) also. (1 John 2:23–23 NKJV, emphasis added) There are no ifs, ands, or buts about it: If you reject Jesus, you are also rejecting God. Why? Because they are the same.

Can you imagine a more destitute picture of someone without Christ, without hope, and without God? This was our pre-Jesus story. It is your story now if you have not accepted Christ as your Savior.

Our Post-Jesus Lives

I am so thankful and encouraged that Ephesians 2:12 is not the end of our story:

> *But now in Christ Jesus* you who once were far off
> have been brought near by the blood of Christ.
> (Ephesians 2:13 NKJV, emphasis added)

In our pre-Jesus days, we were as far away from God as we could possibly be. *But now*, we have been brought near to Him through the blood of Christ. Praise the Lord for the "but now" that we have in the Word of God. Without it, our story does not end well.

Being a child of God means that we have had two birthdays. The first one happened when we were physically born. Most of us have a birth certificate that shows the month, the day, and the year we were born. I know mine: January 10, 1949. The chances are good that you know yours too. Our physical birth is when our pre-Jesus lives began. It is impossible to be *born again* if we were never born the first time. Nicodemus did not understand what Jesus was talking about when He told him that he had to be born again (from above). Nicodemus could only perceive things in the natural realm because he was born disconnected from the spiritual realm. He was without Christ, without hope, and without God.

Nicodemus said to Jesus, "How can a man be born when he is old? Can he enter a *second time* into his mother's womb and be born?" (John 3:4 NKJV). Nicodemus's response to what Jesus said reveals the kind of mindset he had. An individual who has only been born once has physical life, but they are spiritually dead (Psalm 58:3 NKJV). When we are born again, we have both. It is our second birthday that plugs us into the spiritual realm. We are now able to set our minds and affections on things above (Colossians 3:1–4 NKJV). We may live in this world (natural life), but we are not of this world (spiritual life). Here is what Jesus said about those who belong to Him:

> They are not of the world, just as I am not of the world. (John 17:16 NKJV, emphasis added)

The only way to be *in this world* without being *of this world* is to be born from above. This happens when we accept and receive Jesus Christ as our Lord and Savior.

Our spiritual births connect us to the things of the Spirit. We are plugged into the spiritual realm, which cannot be seen by physical eyes or comprehended by natural minds. We have access to things that were inaccessible before. It is possible to think differently because we have new minds. We now have a choice that we did not have before. We can set our minds on the things of this world or on things above. It is our call. I will give you some inside information: If we allow natural thinking to govern our spiritual identities, we are in for some difficult and confusing days as believers.

If the truth of the following passage of scripture ever gets a good hold of you, you will never be the same:

> And we have received God's own Spirit (not the world's spirit), so we can know the wonderful things God has freely given us. When we tell you these things, we do not use words that come from human wisdom (natural mind). Instead, we speak words given to us by the Spirit, using the Spirit's words to explain spiritual truths (spiritual mind). *But people who aren't spiritual can't receive these truths from God's Spirit.* It all sounds foolish to them and *they can't understand what the Spirit means.* Those who are spiritual can evaluate all things, but they themselves cannot be evaluated by others. For, "Who can know the Lord's thoughts? Who knows enough to teach him?" But we understand these things, *for we have the mind of Christ.* (1 Corinthians 2:12–16 NLT, emphasis added).

If you never finish reading this book, I encourage you to pitch your tent and camp in these five verses for as long as it takes for them to transform the way you think as a child of God. We have the mind of Christ. It's time we start using it.

Location, Location, Location

When we were without Christ and without God in our lives, we had no hope. What difference a simple prayer makes. We are made new:

> Therefore, *if anyone is in Christ, he is a new creation*; old things have passed away; behold, *all things have become new.* (2 Corinthians 5:17 NKJV, emphasis added)

All things made new includes a new way of thinking. As new creations, we have the mind of Christ. We need to become aware of who we are and what we possess—and then start thinking like who Christ has made us to be.

Without Jesus, we have nothing. With Jesus, we have everything. We went from having no hope to being full of hope—not by what we do for Him, but by what He did for us. The Lord moved us to a new neighborhood, and He paid for it all with His life.

Location, location, location. This is the mantra used by real estate agents when they talk about the value of homes. It simply means that the value of homes is determined by their location. An appraiser will consider a home's location when they determine property value. It's the location.

What is true in real estate is also true when it comes to one's spiritual location. The quality of life is determined by spiritual location. It is impossible to be in a better spiritual neighborhood than living in Christ:

> For you died to this life, and your real life is hidden with Christ in God. (Colossians 3:3 NLT)

This verse may help us better understand what Jesus meant when He said, "When I am raised to life again, *you will know* that I am in *my Father*, and you are *in me*, and I am *in you*" (John 14:20 NLT, emphasis added).

Process what Jesus said against the backdrop of Ephesians 2:11–12: We were without Christ and without God. Pay close attention to what Jesus said in this passage: He was in the Father. Jesus also said that we are in Him. Then He says He is in us. Has it hit you yet? Since we are in Jesus, and Jesus is in the Father, we are in the Father too. Now that Jesus is in us, and we are in Him, as He is in the Father; the Father is in us. This is why the Word of God says that if we deny Jesus, we do not have the Father either (1 John 2:22–23 NKJV).

God moved us into a new neighborhood. It is the antithesis of the old one Ephesians 2 describes. It was the blood of Christ that made this possible (Ephesians 2:13 NKJV). The property in this neighborhood cannot be purchased by hard works. It is available free of charge to those who are a part of God's forever family. Just because it is free does not mean it is cheap. It cost Jesus everything. He paid the price.

We Were Terrestrial Thinkers

Terrestrial thinking comes from a mind that is set on things in this earthly realm. Our old selves (before Christ) were limited to this earthly realm. Our thoughts were worldly because we were spiritually dead; therefore, our minds were dead to spiritual things. Everything about our old lives was corrupted. We were dead men living; darkened in our understanding, without hope (Ephesians 4:18 NKJV).

By being terrestrial thinkers, we are more inclined to accept human opinions over the Word of God. What we believe is true or not true is based on our experiences. In our pre-Jesus days, the source of our thinking came from the flesh and not the Spirit.

We Are Celestial Thinkers

Celestial thinking comes from a mind that is set on the spiritual realm. As new creations in Christ, we are connected to the Spirit. We are spiritually plugged in. We now have the ability to think like our Creator. If we share His life, we also share His mind. We have the ability to think like the new creations we are in Christ—now that we are partakers of His divine nature (2 Peter 1:4 NKJV).

The freedom of choice belongs to us. We choose where we focus our minds. If we set our minds on the flesh, we will find ourselves living by the flesh (Romans 8:5 NKJV). If we set our minds on the Spirit, we will find ourselves walking in the Spirit (Romans 8:5 NKJV):

> For to be carnally minded (flesh) is death, but to be *spiritually minded is life and peace.* (Romans 8:6 NKJV, emphasis added)

What is humanity searching for? The very thing that only the spiritually minded will find: life and peace.

It's Time We Start Thinking Like New Creations

When we start thinking like the new creations we are, we will start behaving in accordance. We behave wrong because we believe wrong. We must never underestimate the power of our thought lives. Here is a really good rework of one of Ralph Waldo Emerson's famous quotes I read recently:

> Watch your thoughts, for they become words. Watch your words, for they become actions. Watch your actions, for they become habits. Watch your

habits, for they become character. Watch your character, for it becomes your destiny.

Our destinies are determined by thoughts.

God is the only one who can bring peace to your past, purpose to your present, and hope to your future. Trust Him. The one who was alive (Jesus) died, so the ones who were dead (us) can be made alive.

Lillian Dickson said, "Life is like a coin. You can spend it anyway you wish, but you only spend it once." For a person to be eternally separated from God, they will have to stumble into outer darkness over His unconditional love. He loves you too much to force you to love Him back.

CHAPTER 5

WE WERE FOREORDAINED TO REIGN IN THIS LIFE

G od had a specific purpose in His creation of humanity. And in spite of humanity's disobedience and rebellion against Him, His purpose remains intact. God intended humanity to reign with Him in this life:

> Then the Lord said, "*Let us make human beings in our image*, to be like us. *They will reign* over the fish in the sea, the birds in the sky, the livestock, all the wild animals on the earth, and the small animals that scurry along the ground." (Genesis 1:26 NLT, emphasis added)

God foreordained human beings to reign with Him in the natural realm as He reigns in the spiritual realm. This was God's plan from the very beginning of time, and it has not changed. Ruling and reigning with Christ in this earthly realm will challenge normal Christian thinking.

Our Earthly Assignment

God's preordained plan is for human beings to express and present Him here in the earthly realm. Being successful in this heavenly assignment requires new creation thinking. If we are to reign like Christ, we must think like Him—and we can. This ability was given to us the moment we had our born-from-above encounter with the Lord. As new creation beings, we have the capacity to think differently than we did before our salvation experiences (1 Corinthians 2:16 NLT).

The citizenry of the kingdom of heaven is made up of kings (Revelation 1:6 NKJV). The moment we accepted the Lord's invitation to life, we were made kings—by the King. Jesus called this moment being born from above (John 3:3 NKJV). Spiritually speaking, we had a second birthday, which gave us the rights and privileges of kingdom citizens. We are no longer citizens of this world. This is no longer our homeland. We may still be in this world, but we are not of this world (John 17:15–16 NKJV).

God assigned us the task of representing Him and His kingdom to the inhabitants of this world:

> So *we are Christ's ambassadors*; *God is making his appeal through us. We speak for Christ* when we plead, "Come back to God!" (2 Corinthians 5:20 NLTV emphasis added)

We are Christ's ambassadors. An ambassador is a diplomatic agent of the highest rank, appointed to represent their government. They do not represent themselves; therefore, they do not have the liberty to express their own opinions about governmental policies. This is why ambassadors say, "The position of my government is," and then they give their government's stance. If an ambassador violates this protocol, they will be recalled—and they should be.

We have been appointed by our Creator to represent heaven's

government in this earthly realm. We do not have the right to our own opinions about heaven's policies. The only thing we are allowed to say is this: "The position of my kingdom government is." We should then quote the scriptures. The Word of God is our Constitution. What the world has to say is not worth a hill of beans if it contradicts the Word of God. If we begin to espouse our own opinions instead of what our government's policies are, we are subject to recall. I wonder how many of us have been recalled and are not even aware of it.

We Were Born to Reign in This Life

> For if by one man's offense *death reigned* through the one (first Adam), much more those who receive abundance of grace and of the gift of righteousness *will reign in life* through the One, Jesus Christ (last Adam). (Romans 5:17 NKJV, emphasis added)

We must never forget that our marching orders come from the Word of God. Since we are His ambassadors, representing His kingdom, we do not have the right to our own opinions about what His position is on anything. He means what He says, and He says what He means. And He says in this passage that we are to reign in this life. It's high time we start. This will not happen until we start thinking like who He has made us to be. It will take a kingdom mindset.

Humanity's earthly assignment has not changed since it was given in Genesis 1:26–28 (NKJV). One of the first things Jesus stressed when He began His public ministry was the necessity for us to change the way we think. He reminds us of our purpose for being in this earthly realm:

> From that time Jesus began to preach and to say, *"Repent, for the kingdom of heaven is at hand."* (Matthew 4:17 NKJV, emphasis added)

Pay close attention to the announcement Jesus made: The unseen kingdom of heaven can now be seen in the earthly realm. In other words, the government of heaven is on the scene. The rule of God has arrived on earth.

The Greek word for *repent* is *metanoia*. It means to change one's mind. It is literally a change of heart. If we are to understand heaven's government, God's rule, it will require a different mindset than we had before. We must change the way we think. Since we are citizens of heaven, we need to start thinking like heavenly citizens.

We need to be careful and not confuse *repenting* with *confessing*. It is possible to confess but not repent. How many times have you heard someone say, "I've repented over and over, but I still have not gotten victory." That is when they name their struggles. This is the problem. They have confessed, but they have not repented. When we repent (change the way we think about sin), we enjoy more freedom from sin. Repenting is seeing things the way God sees them. When we see sin the way God does, we will sin less.

The Word of God states unequivocally that old creation thinking cannot comprehend heaven's government or the rule of God. The natural mind is not plugged into the power source, and it cannot be connected because it is not wired for it. It will require repentance, a different way of thinking. As new creations, we have the ability to think differently, see things differently, and live differently.

Let me repeat what I just said and add an addendum to it: Heaven's government cannot be understood with the natural mind or by normal Christianity. We will not be effective ambassadors if we keep thinking like worldly citizens. That is who we used to be. It is not who we are. As new creations in Christ, we are in this world—but we are not of this world. We have the mind of Christ because we are partakers of His divine nature (1 Corinthians 2:16 NKJV, 2 Peter 1:4 NKJV).

It Is Time to Start Reigning

Reigning begins by knowing our identities as children of God and understanding that we are co-laborers with God. Reigning is not about having a position of authority on the outside; it is about having control over what is on the inside. This is why I began this book by talking about living life from the inside out. If we are to exercise the authority given to us by our heavenly Father, it will require us to live our lives from the inside out. We must always keep on the front burner of our minds that we are kings living in a kingdom of kings, co-laboring with the King of kings. As kings, we do not rule over other kings. We don't lord it over other people. The kingdom of God does not have cosmic cops—self-appointed spiritual law officers out searching for violators. This is not reigning. This is ruling.

Keep in mind what God's purpose is for our lives. We are to express and present Him to this earthly realm. To do this effectively, we must always keep our focus on Him. When we do, we will love people the way He does; when we love people the way He does, we will minister to people the way He does. This is a snapshot of what it looks like to co-labor with God (1 Corinthians 3:9 NKJV). We must be so heavenly minded that we are of earthly good.

One thing for certain is that we will never reign if we don't know we can. Normal Christianity does not think so. That in no way suggests that the average believer does not think there will not be some victories and overcoming moments in their lives, but it will not be a lifestyle. Normal Christianity thinks we will reign someday—but not today. Everything is distance and delay for the majority of the community of faith. Their mindset is totally focused on the sweet by-and-by, but our assignment is to reign in the nasty now-and-now. All you have to do is listen to how people talk and watch how they live their lives to find out what they actually believe about their identities as children of God—and how much authority they believe they have.

The Passion Translation of Romans 5:17 is so colorful:

Death once held us in its grip, and by the blunder of one man (Adam), death reigned as king over humanity. But now, how much more are we held in the grip of grace and continue reigning as kings in life, enjoying our regal freedom through the gift of perfect righteousness in the one and only Jesus, the Messiah (emphasis added).

The following quote from an unknown author presents us with a sobering truth: "Death is just a change of address, but what you believe will determine what neighborhood you end up in." What neighborhood will you be moving to? Moving day is coming.

Always Triumphant—More than Conquerors

Now thanks be to God who *always leads us in triumph in Christ*, and through us diffuses the fragrance of His knowledge in every place. (2 Corinthians 2:14 NKJV, emphasis added)

Once again, we see our purpose for being in this earthly realm. God expresses Himself through us as we present Him to those in our circles of influence. God lives in us—to express Himself through us—as us (1 Corinthians 6:19 NKJV).

The Word of God also declares that we are always victorious in Christ. This would be much easier to digest if Paul had said that we are triumphant *sometimes* or even *most of the time*. But always! What about those times we stepped out of our comfort zones, attempted to do exploits for God, and fell short? When this happens, we need to capture our thoughts and not allow our experiences to define what is true and not true instead of trusting the Word of God. Our experiences are real, but they are not necessarily true. God's Word says that we always win, and His Word is always true (John 17:17 NKJV).

When we allow the Spirit of God to govern us from within, no matter what happens outside of us, we are able to stay in His perfect peace. There will be times when things do not turn out the way we were hoping or thought they would turn out, but that doesn't mean we failed. God can continue to express Himself through us as we present Him to those around us. "You will keep him in perfect peace, Whose mind is stayed on You" (Isaiah 26:3 NKJV).

No matter what happens to us in life, we need to keep our minds set on Him. When things are not going as we think they should, as long as we keep our minds focused on Him, we stay in peace. Because Christ is our peace (Ephesians 2:14 NKJV), we win! If we don't see ourselves as always being victorious in Christ, then our focus is not where it should be. We are focusing on the circumstances that surround us instead of the truth within us. Reigning is an inward condition and not an outward position. When we win on the inside, we will never see ourselves as losers on the outside.

The Word of God tells us that we are always victorious and that we are more than conquerors:

> Yet in all these things *we are more than conquerors* through Him who loved us. (Romans 8:37 NKJV, emphasis added)

We are always victorious in Him, and we are more than conquerors through Him. Life is all about Him. We are in Him, and He is in us (John 14:20 NKJV). There is no life apart from God. If this is true, then why don't we live like it? It could be because we have a thinking problem. This is outside the parameters of normal Christianity. This is why so many kingdom citizens live as victims and not as victors. God has appointed us to be His ambassadors and represent heaven's government here on the earth, but we are not thinking like ambassadors.

Our Greatest Challenge

The greatest challenge for the community of faith is not getting the unredeemed out of this world's system; it is getting this world's system out of the redeemed. The toughest battle we face does not come from without; it comes from within. Even though we are new creations in Christ, we still struggle with old creation thinking. We know Christ has brought us out of this world, but most people are not willing to allow Him to take the world out of them. This makes it impossible for us to reign in this life. Reigning is not going to be experienced by a child of God who still thinks like they did when they were an unbeliever. Old creation thinking will not work in the new creation mind because it is not designed to. Are you still who you used to be—or have you been made brand-new? It is time to start thinking like who we are in Christ so we can begin to reign in this life.

Old nature thinking is the petri dish where all sorts of unhealthy thoughts breed. Left unchecked, they will ultimately lead to living a life that is far below God's intention for His children. Make no mistake about it—you will live the way you think.

Paul stresses the importance of abandoning our old way of thinking in his letter to the Christians who lived in Rome:

> And *do not be conformed* to this world, but *be transformed* by the *renewing of our mind,* that you *may prove* what is that good and acceptable and perfect will of God. (Romans 12:2 NKJV, emphasis added)

In this verse, we are presented with two ways of thinking. We can allow the world to conform our thinking—and the Word of God warns us against that—or we can allow God to transform our thinking. Again, we have a choice.

Think about the word *conform* for a moment. Let's separate this word into two parts. The prefix *con* means with or together. The word *form* means to mold, shape, fashion, or form. The Word of God warns us not to allow the world to form, shape, or mold our thinking. Jesus told us we are in the world, but we are not of the world (John 17:15–16 NKJV). If we are not of the world, then we should not be thinking like the world. This is why there is so much misbehavior within the Christian community today. They know they are not of the world, but they still think like the world. This is a recipe for living a defeated life, but it also keeps us from ever knowing our birthrights and privileges as children of God's forever family. The old way of thinking will keep us from living up to our calling (Ephesians 4:1 NLT).

Most of the time, too many Christians are still thinking the same way they did before they had their come-to-Jesus moment. The danger in that is that most of them are not even aware of it. This is one of those situations when ignorance is not bliss.

Instead of being *conformed* by the world, we are to be *transformed* by the renewing of our minds. The Greek word for *transform* is *metamorphoo*. It is a compound verb comprised of *meta*, implying change, and *morphe,* meaning form. Transformation emphasizes a total change from the inside out.

Let's connect some dots. When you had your born-from-above experience with Christ, you became a new creation (2 Corinthians 5:17 NKJV). God did not renovate the old you and bring you up to spiritual code; He made you a brand-new creation. Since you are a completely new person, your old way of thinking (worldly) is not designed or equipped to function in the new you. Your mind, the way you think, must be transformed. This happens when we constantly set our minds on heavenly things (Colossians 3:1–4 NKJV). This transformation will begin to express itself through our character and conduct. It is an inside-out process. When this happens, we are equipped and ready to reign in this life.

As our minds are being transformed, we will be able to recognize God's perfect will, which is good, pleasing, and perfect (Romans

12:2 NKJV). We will find it much easier to allow God to express Himself through us as we present Him to those around us.

Reigning from the Inside Out

The story of Joseph gives us some invaluable insights into what reigning in life looks like. Most believers are familiar with his story. I strongly suggest you read it if you have not, and if you have, I encourage you to read it again. It is found in Genesis 37–50. Even though Joseph was a brash and conceited seventeen-year-old young man, he did not deserve the treatment he received from his brothers, the Ishmaelite slave traders, or Potiphar's wife.

Because Joseph never lost his focus, God took him from the pit, from Potiphar's house, from prison, and made him the prime minister of Egypt—and he was a Jew. He was able to go from the "gutter-most" to the "uttermost" because he never shifted his focus away from God. Joseph refused to allow his outside position to affect his inside condition. I wonder how many promotions we may have forfeited simply because we were more fixated on what was happening to us than on what God has done in us.

Here is something I find very interesting: Not much is said about how Joseph ruled over the people of Egypt. We do know that he was given free rein by Pharaoh (Genesis 41:41–46 NKJV). The majority of his story is spent showing us how he reigned over lust and how he dealt with his brothers who had sold him into slavery. He ruled effectively in the land of Egypt because he had learned how to rule the land that was inside of him.

If Joseph could do it, we can too. The Spirit of God does not abide *on us* like He did with Joseph. The Spirit of God lives *within us* and has promised never to leave or forsake us (Hebrews 13:5 NKJV). There is so much angst in most Christians today because they have bought into the lie that things will never be any different, and they will never have victory over a besetting sin. We need to rise up and take our stand on the Word of God. God's purpose for humanity in the beginning has not changed or been altered. We have been foreordained to reign in this life.

I am fairly confident that most Christians believe we will reign with Christ in heaven someday (Revelation 20:4–6 NKJV). The emphasis is on *someday*. This is the distant-and-delay theology that is so pervasive in normal Christianity. We know we will reign with Him in the sweet by-and-by, but we are not certain we can reign with Him in the here and now. The Word that says we will reign with Christ in heaven is the same word that says we are to reign in this life (Romans 5:17 NKJV). Our inward condition will determine our outward position.

The following quote from John Wesley sums up this entire chapter in a clear and concise way: "Whosoever will reign with Christ in heaven must have Christ reigning in him on earth." Thank you, Mr. J. W.

CHAPTER 6

GIGO THINKING

I vividly remember when the computer era was getting traction. To keep their pastor "in the world of know," some men in my church gifted me a very nice computer system. Even though I was deeply appreciative for what they had done for me, I was not overjoyed by their gift. I had no clue how to turn it on or off. People who know me the best know how technologically challenged I am. Okay. I will go ahead and be transparent; most technology intimidates me. Please don't ask me why because I am not sure I know.

I was assured by these generous, kindhearted men that I would catch on fairly easily, and they were right—to a degree. It did not take long for me to grasp the basic requirements to operate my computer: turning it on and off, typing a letter, you know, the biggies. Even though the computer belonged to me, I did not know all of the incredible benefits that were at my fingertips. It would not have mattered if I had known because I did not know how to access them.

Then, while I was pecking on my keyboard, I had a brainstorm. My beloved wife says my brainstorms are really only small blows. She is usually right. My idea was to call the seminary I had attended years earlier to see if they had a computer class that I could take. Sure enough, they did.

I asked which professor was teaching the class, and when they told me, I was excited and relieved at the same time. It was one of my favorite professors from years back. I immediately knew this was a God thing because when they transferred my call to his office, he was the one who answered the phone, not his secretary. After a few minutes of catching up on our lives, I told him what I was looking for. I needed a class where computer basics were taught. I told him about my computer phobia, and he assured me that his class was designed for people like me. In all the years I have known this great man of God, it was the first time he had ever lied to me.

When I walked into his classroom, fear almost took me to my knees. I saw wall-to-wall computers. The entire room was full of intimidation. After a brief introduction, each student was assigned a computer that would be theirs for the entire semester. It only took about ten minutes of classroom time to realize that I was out of my league. My used-to-be professor friend began to write all kinds of symbols, letters, numbers, codes, and other unrecognizable characters on the chalkboard, and I had never seen any of them before. Yes, this was back in the day of chalkboards. I immediately knew that I had missed God's will for my computer life.

I would have needed a degree in computer science to be able to access the monster that was sitting on a desk before me. I was looking for basic computer information—basics! I can't tell you how many times my screen went blank after I had poked and punched numbers and symbols in an attempt to gain access. It took me about a month to finally get a grasp of how to get where I needed to be in the computer. And once I was able to get it open, I was no better off. I did not know where to go from there. It took another month to be able to do that. Thank goodness the semester would soon be over. I fought the urge to quit on several occasions, but quitting is not in my nature. I hung in there, but hanging was about all I could do.

One day, my computer and I were at odds with one another. When I entered something into my computer, I was getting a bunch of junk in return. Puzzled, I asked my former friend for help. He said something that I had not heard in a long time. "When you put garbage into your computer, that is exactly what you are going to get in return: Garbage in, garbage out. A computer will only process what you put into it."

This brief story about my computer illiteracy is the unadulterated truth. I have taken no license in sharing my story. Here is my purpose for telling you: Your mind is an incredible computer. What you put in it will determine what comes out. If you put garbage in, guess what you will get in return. Keep this in mind as you continue reading about GIGO thinking.

Let me put this in biblical language: You will always get what you sow:

> Do not be deceived, God is not mocked; for *whatever a man sows, that he will also reap.* (Galatians 6:7 NKJV, emphasis added)

It should be mandatory that this passage of scripture be inscribed on every computer sold.

Satanic Cyberattacks

Satanic cyberattacks are perpetrated against God's children on a daily basis, and he uses this world's system as his main weapon because it is corrupt to the core. Our computer minds are infiltrated every day by the enemy. Most of the time, we are not even aware that we are being victimized as our thought lives are constantly bombarded with unhealthy input. Satan is adept at disrupting, disabling, destroying, and maliciously controlling our thought lives. His goal is to destroy the integrity of our thinking.

If Satan ever succeeds in controlling the ways we think, he can control the ways we live. He knows our thoughts are the hardware that determines how we conduct ourselves. He is very aware of the GIGO principle. The environment he is most skilled is in the infrastructure of our minds. Even though he cannot read our minds, he can sow thoughts—and if we do not take them captive, there can be devastating consequences.

I cannot think of a better example to illustrate this than King Saul. King Saul had mustered his army near the Valley of Elah to engage the Philistine army. Try to picture this scene in your mind. The Philistine army was positioned on the hills facing the Valley of Elah, while the Israelites stood on the opposite side of the valley facing the Philistines. These two armies were having a face-off.

As they are sizing up the strength of their foe, all of a sudden, a behemoth of a man standing nine feet tall, steps out from the Philistine ranks and into the valley, and he begins to challenge the Israelite army. All of the macho chattering coming from the Israelite side grows deafeningly silent. There is no line of volunteers forming from the Israelite army to take on this dude:

> When Saul and the Israelites heard this, they were terrified and deeply shaken. (1 Samuel 17:11 NLT)

This challenging situation went on for forty days. I find this interesting because forty is the number for testing in the scriptures. It was certainly a test.

The moment of engagement arrives, and both armies run down into the valley with shouts and battle cries. The armies are standing face-to-face. The huge Philistine warrior steps to the front and draws a line in the sand. His sheer size frightens everyone on the Israelite side. The Israelite army thought Goliath was big from a distance, but standing face-to-face with him silences their smack-talking:

> As soon as the Israelites saw him, *they began to run away in fright*. (1 Samuel 17:24 NLT, emphasis added)

As the men run away, the future king of Israel steps to the forefront. He is the youngest son of Jesse, the Bethlehemite. His name is David. David is totally ignorant about what had been going on. He is just being obedient to his father's instructions to bring food to his brothers.

I want to cut to the chase so we can spend time on what was happening in the thought life of King Saul. You can read the entire story in 1 Samuel 16–30. This was the moment Satan's malware gained access to Saul's computer (his thought life). A thought was planted that would ultimately end in his death and the death of his three sons.

David was able to do what the Israelite army had failed to accomplish. He did not measure himself by the size of his enemy. He measured his enemy by the size of his God. With a sling and a smooth stone, David took out Goliath. This one heroic act landed him a position of authority in Saul's military.

First Samuel 18:6 begins with these words: "Now it happened" (NKJV). Those three words alert us to Satan's scheme: You sow, you reap.

> When the victorious Israelite army was returning home after David had killed the Philistine, women from all the towns of Israel came out with tambourines and cymbals. This was their song: "Saul has killed his thousands, and David his ten thousands!" This made Saul very angry. "What's this?" he said. "They credit David with ten thousands and me with only thousands. *Next they'll be making him their king!*" So from that time on, Saul kept a jealous eye on David. (1 Samuel 18: 8 NLT, emphasis added)

Who was Saul talking to? This conversation was taking place between his ears—in his mind. Where did these thoughts of David wanting to be king come from? The enemy seized this moment to plant the seed of jealously in the mind of Saul. He just knew David was after his throne. Thoughts only have the life you give them. David was not after the kingdom. He just woke up one morning and killed a giant.

I shared this brief story of King Saul's life because the enemy has not changed his tactics. He still tries to influence the way we live by planting thoughts that are not true. He wants to convince us that we own these thoughts and that they originated within us. He is a liar and the father of all lies. There is no truth in him whatsoever (John 8:44 NKJV). As long as we are in this world, we will always have to deal with Satanic cyberattacks.

Defense against Satanic cyberattacks

> For our weapons (Malwarebytes) of our warfare are not carnal but mighty in God for pulling down strongholds, casting down arguments and every high thing that exalts itself against the knowledge of God, *bringing every thought into captivity* to the obedience of Christ. (2 Corinthians 10:4–5 NKJV, emphasis added)

Paul tells us in this verse that we are to capture rebellious thoughts and teach them to obey Christ. Is this possible? Would God tell us to do something that was impossible to do? Does God want us to have healthy thought lives? As new creations, we are divinely wired to bring into captivity every thought that passes between our ears. This does not mean that bad thoughts will cease to come; we cannot control that. However, we do have absolute control over how long those thoughts stay in our heads. Let me quote Martin Luther again: "You cannot keep birds from flying over your head, but you do have the power to keep them from building a nest in your hair." Our spiritual cybersecurity is impenetrable by Satan's constant probing.

And that is truth, which is the Word of God. Truth will protect us from Satan's unending attempts to access our thought lives. With Christ, all things are possible (Matthew 19:26 NKJV).

Protection against attacks on our thought lives does not come without effort on our part. We are not spiritual robots. Even though we have everything needed to protect what thoughts stay in our minds, we have to activate it. This must be done on purpose. This must be intentional on our part.

Everyone knows the best defense is a good offense, and this is really true when it comes to new creation thinking. The best way to protect yourself against unhealthy thoughts is to be proactive. This is what Paul tells the church in Philippi:

> And now, dear brothers and sisters, one final thing. *Fix your thoughts* on what is true, and honorable, and right, and pure, and lovely, and admirable. *Think about things* that are excellent and worthy of praise. (Philippians 4:8 NLT, emphasis added)

Fixing our thoughts on what is true—and thinking about things that are excellent—speaks to our responsibility. This will not happen automatically.

The Word of God does not teach positive thinking, but it does go to great depths about thinking positively. We should live by what the scriptures say and not by what we hear in some positive-thinking symposium:

> Since you have been raised to *a new life* with Christ, *set your sights* (mind) on the realities of heaven, where Christ sits in the place of honor at God's right hand. *Think about the things of heaven*, not the things of earth. For you died to this life, and *your real life* (new creation) is hidden with Christ in God. (Colossians 3:1–3 NLT, emphasis added)

It is worth noting that living a life of peace follows thinking about peaceful things:

> *Keep putting into practice* all you learned and received from me—everything you heard from me and *saw me doing.* Then *the God of peace will be with you.* (Philippians 4:9 NLT, emphasis added)

One translation says that we are to practice these things. I find it interesting that doing right comes after thinking right. When we think right, we behave right. When we behave right, we enjoy the fruit of peace. This is the formula for living a life of peace.

To encourage their teams to give nothing less than their best in game preparation, coaches say, "You will play the way you practice." What is true in sports is true when it comes to living a victorious life on this side of eternity. You will live the way you think. The enemy of your soul knows that. This is why he is so relentless in his attacks in the realm of our thoughts. If he can't get you to believe a lie, he will twist the truth in an attempt to get you to believe that a half-truth is the whole truth. It never has been, and it will never be.

Don't Own What's Not Yours

This would be a good time to repeat the first sentence in the introduction of this book: "It takes faith and a lot of courage to walk away from normal Christianity." This section will show you how true that statement really is.

When Christ died and rose from the dead, Satan was not wounded or severely injured. He was totally and completely defeated. Jesus did not come into this world to cohabit with the devil. He came to destroy his works (1 John 3:8 NKJV). Have you ever totaled a vehicle or seen one that has been totaled? Being totaled means it is beyond repair. You can sit in it and pretend you're driving, but you are not going anywhere. You can't because the vehicle no longer has the ability to operate like it did before it was rendered inoperable. This is a picture of what Jesus did to the enemy of our souls. He totaled him and rendered him of no effect. The devil does not have the ability to do anything without permission. He is still around, but he can't bite us anymore because God pulled out his fangs on Calvary's cross. We need to stop allowing him to gum us to death.

Some of the most vile and ungodly thoughts have flashed through my mind while I was in a worship service or when I was about to stand up and preach the Word. If you don't know the source of these filthy thoughts, you will own them as yours. Once you take ownership, the little chirping voices in your head will begin to serenade you with songs like these: "How can you love God and entertain thoughts like that?" "You are such a hypocrite." "How can God love someone who has thoughts like you just had?" "You should be ashamed of yourself because God is." If the devil can convince you that these thoughts are yours, guilt will cover you like a heavy coat. Never forget what the Word of God calls him: a liar (John 8:44 NKJV).

The Word of God tells us that we have become new persons in Christ; our old lives are gone, and our new lives have begun (2 Corinthians 5:17 NLT). If we never discover this "new person" that we have become in Christ, we will never live lives of victory with any consistency. Knowing who you are in Christ is tantamount to being more than a conqueror (Romans 8:37 NKJV).

Most Christians see themselves as physical beings who have spirits, but the opposite is true. We are spiritual beings who have souls, and we live in physical bodies. These bodies of flesh will return to the dust someday, but our spirits will live on. On that day, we will be given glorified bodies for our spirits to live in. Until then, even though we are new creations, we will continue to live in these old earthly suits assigned to us at our first birthday. This is where most of the confusion about our new identities stems from. We are more focused on our physical conditions than we are on our spiritual conditions. You are a spiritual being—who has a soul—and you live in a body. Your physical body is not the eternal part of you. It came from dirt, and it will return to the dirt.

In the moment you surrendered your life to Jesus Christ, you became a new person. Old things passed away, and all things became new (2 Corinthians 5:17 NKJV). When the Word says that old things passed away and everything was made new, that is exactly what it means. God did not bring the old you up to date. He did not remodel or renovate you. You became a brand-new creation. There is none of the old you left in the new you. If there was, you would not be a completely new creation. This is something the enemy hopes you never discover. He knows how difficult it will be to manufacture evidence to accuse you with when you discover the old you no longer exists. The old you died long before whatever the enemy accuses you of doing. And he knows this (Romans 6:6 NKJV). If I am convinced that my new identity cohabits with my old identity, then the only thing I can believe is that these ungodly thoughts do come from within. I own them. Since I own them, I must work harder so I won't have as many vulgar thoughts in the future. It is a revolving door; it is always going around, but it's going nowhere.

If the old person that we were no longer exists, then what is the source of the unhealthy thoughts that flash through our minds on occasions? These thoughts are the devil's darts. They come from the voice of the enemy. He is the source. We do not detect it is him because we have heard it all our lives, and because of this, we assume these thoughts are ours. This scam is not something new. It originated in Genesis 3 when Satan planted seeds of rebellion in the thoughts of Adam and Eve. He has not altered his scheme. Why fix something if it works? GIGO.

What do you do when you are being bombarded with ungodly thoughts? I am glad you asked. Victory begins with knowledge. Since you are a new creation in Christ, these ungodly thoughts cannot be yours; so, don't own what is not yours. This would be a good place for you to shout. Once you declare this truth, you issue a cease and desist order against your enemy. Begin by thanking the Lord for being your life (Acts 17:28 NKJV). Then throw the Word of God in the devil's face. You do this by lifting up your voice in praise and openly declaring your identity as a child of God. Remind yourself that these are not your thoughts, and they have no legal right to intrude on your thought life. Thank the Lord that because you have His mind, you can think His thoughts (1 Corinthians 2:16 NKJV). Intentionally set your mind and affections on things that are above (Colossians 3:2 NKJV). This is how you capture your thoughts.

Have you noticed that I have said very little about talking to the enemy? Let me tell you why. Far too many Christians spend more time rebuking the devil than they do talking to God. Spend intimate time talking with your heavenly Father, and His presence will rebuke the devil. Your victory is in Christ and Christ alone. The enemy cannot enter the holy of holies. If he could, he would get saved. Since Christ is in the Father—and you are in Him, and He is in you—you're on holy ground (John 14:20 NKJV). It is time to discover who we are and whose we are.

If Satan has attacked your identity as a child of God, that is an indication that you are a child of God. Being attacked is normal. The enemy is very deceitful, but he is only effective against those who are unaware or unprepared (Hebrews 2:14–15; Colossians 1:13). Your fight is not with people. Your battle is against demonic darkness. This is spiritual warfare. Fight to win.

Mark Twain said, "What a wee little part of a person's life are his acts and his words! His real life is led in his head and is known to none but himself. All day long, the mill of his brain is grinding, and his thoughts, not those other things, are his history."

CHAPTER 7

DISCOVERING OUR NEW SELVES

———

W hy does normal Christianity have no problem accepting what the scriptures say about Jesus and His identity, but colic over what the word says about our identities as new creation beings. We are the offspring of the last Adam's (Jesus) incorruptible seed. Could it be because of our experiences? It is possible that we are not living up to who the scriptures say we are. New creation identity is difficult to embrace because our tendency is to define truth based on our experiences when we should be allowing the Word of God, which is truth, to validate or invalidate our experiences. Knowingly or unknowingly, we allow our experiences to be the thesaurus that defines our identity. Here is the zinger: Our experiences may be real, but they may not be true.

You may be thinking, *Is it really that important to know more than I do about my new creation identity?* The enemy of your soul knows how important it is. This is why he fights so hard to conceal the truth about who you are now that you have had a second birthday. So many Christians have settled with knowing they have been redeemed, and when it's all said and done here on earth, they will go to heaven. Those are good things to know, but there is so much more to what we have in Christ. Because our experiences are so real and personal, they challenge the legitimacy of what the scriptures say about our new creation identities.

Will it make that much of a difference in how we live our daily lives if we are able to see our new selves the way our Creator sees us? The difference will be nothing less than shocking. Because we are so connected to our physical surroundings—a world corrupted by Adam's sin of disobedience—we live with a subliminal assumption that the physical realm is more real than the spiritual realm. And we believe that we are more physical than we are spiritual, but the complete opposite is true. We are spiritual beings living in physical bodies. Our physical bodies are temporary. Our spirits are eternal.

Finding Ourselves

When I use the term *new selves*, I am not talking about our physical makeup. I am talking about the new creations we have become in Christ. This is a challenge because our new lives are lived through our old bodies. Our bodies are nothing more than earth suits that make it legal for us to be in this earthly realm. Once these bodies succumb to the limitations of this physical life, they will return to the dust from whence they came. They will become worm food. When this happens, our real selves—the new creations we have become in Christ—will begin to enjoy the reality of the eternal realm.

Where does one go to discover their new self? Since Jesus is our example for everything, let's look to Him. Where did He go? What did He do? Luke 3–4 holds the answer to our questions. Luke records the launching of Jesus's public ministry, beginning with His baptism:

> When all the people were baptized, it came to
> pass that Jesus also was baptized; and while He

> prayed, the heaven was opened. And the Holy Spirit descended in bodily form like a dove upon Him, and a voice came from heaven which said, *"You are My beloved Son; in You I am well pleased."* (Luke 3:21–22 NKJV, emphasis added)

Let's slow-roll what Luke is telling us because it will give us a deeper insight into Satan's hubris in attacking the identity of the Son of God. He uses the same tactic of spiritual warfare that he used on the Son of God on the children of God. It will be advantageous for us to pay close attention to what Jesus did and said when Satan attacked His identity. If the devil can scam you out of your *new self identity*, he will be able to steal your birthright privileges as well:

> This is My beloved Son; in You I am well pleased. (Luke 3:22 NKJV)

What work had Jesus preformed at this juncture of his life and ministry that caused God to say, "I am well pleased?" I will give you the answer—not one. God the Father was pleased because Jesus was His Son. This is very significant. When God spoke from heaven and declared His joy over Jesus being His Son, the enemy heard it as well. The devil knows the voice of God. Before his rebellion against his Creator, he was an anointed cherub that possibly led worship in heaven. He was familiar with the voice of God (Ezekiel 28:12–19; Isaiah 14:12–15 NKJV).

The devil spent forty days probing, prodding, and tempting Jesus. At the end of this forty-day period, Jesus was hungry. This is when the devil said to Him, *"If you are the Son of God,* command these stones to become bread" (Luke 4:3 NKJV, emphasis added). When Jesus began His public ministry, Satan immediately attacked His identity. Most translations use the word *if,* which creates doubt. Maybe you are the Son of God, maybe not. A few translations use the word *since,* a subtle attempt to get Jesus to use his identity to satisfy His fleshly need. Since you are the Son of God, and you are hungry, turn this rock in to a loaf of bread. Using the word *if* or *since* does not change the fact that Satan attacked Jesus's identity. Jesus did not take a bite of Satan's bait. The serpent is fishing with the same lure he used to snare Adam and Eve in Genesis 3. Since it worked on the first Adam, maybe it will work on the last Adam (1 Corinthians 15:45 NKJV).

Satan was relentless in his attack on Jesus. Each time Satan would make a suggestion in an attempt to snare Him, Jesus would say, "It is written." He would then quote the written Word of God. This is so crucial to understanding who we are as new creations in Christ: our new selves. This is what the enemy of your soul tries so hard to conceal from you. He wants to keep you away from the written Word of God so you will never discover the new you.

After this forty-day temptation period, full of the Holy Spirit, Jesus returned to Nazareth, where He spent His childhood. Since it was the Sabbath, He did what He always did on this special day; He went to the synagogue:

> And He was handed the book of the prophet Isaiah. And when He had opened the book, *He found the place* where it was written: The Spirit of *the Lord is upon Me*, Because *He has anointed Me* to preach the gospel to the poor; *He has sent Me* to heal the brokenhearted, to proclaim liberty to the captives and recovery of sight to the blind, to set at liberty those who are oppressed; to proclaim the acceptable year of the Lord. (Luke 4:17–18 NKJV, emphasis added)

I find it interesting that Jesus did not read the last sentence of Isaiah 61:2 to His captive audience: "And the day of vengeance of our God" (NKJV). Why did He not read these words? Because it was a day of grace—not vengeance. The day of vengeance is coming!

After reading from Isaiah 61, Jesus handed the scroll back to the attendant and sat down. Every eye in the synagogue was fixed on Him. They were mesmerized and taken aback by the gracious words that flowed from His mouth:

> Then he began to speak to them. "The Scripture you've just heard has been fulfilled this very day." (Luke 4:21 NLT)

In other words, Jesus is saying that the passage He read to them from Isaiah 61 was speaking about Him: This is Me. Jesus, the Living Word, found His identity in the written Word of God. The congregants were amazed at what He said:

> And they said, *"Is this not Joseph's son?"* (Luke 4:22 NKJV, emphasis added)

If we do not allow the Word of God to identify who we are in Christ, the world will be more than happy to oblige us.

Do not forget the two questions we posed earlier. Where do we go to discover our identities as new creations? It is true that Jesus went to the local synagogue, but more importantly, he went to the written Word of God:

> Jesus *found the place* where it was written. (Luke 4:17 NKJV, emphasis added)

Jesus allowed the scriptures to disclose His identity to those in attendance on that Sabbath Day. This is the same place we must go to *find* our identities. What does the written Word of God say about us? What do our new selves look like? The scriptures give us the answer to this question. This is why Jesus told us to remain in His Word (John 8:31–32 NKJV).

What do we do after we discover who we are in Christ? We

begin by confessing (saying the same thing) what the Word of God says about us. This may be awkward for most Christians at first because it steps outside the parameters of normal Christianity, and most of the time, it flies in the face of our experiences. We think, *Since our experiences are real, they must be true, right?* Wrong. Just because our experiences are real, it does not mean they are true. We must expose our experiences to the truth of the Word of God to determine whether they are true or not.

Let me give you one linchpin example. This one sentence keeps the community of faith anchored to the natural realm and makes it difficult to enjoy our new selves. "I'm just a sinner saved by grace." Since I am saved—and I do sin—it makes sense that I am a sinner who is saved by grace. Why does the Word of God have to make sense to us before we embrace and confess it? If we believe that we are sinners who are saved by grace, we are allowing our experiences to define our identities—and not the Word of God. The truth is that we are saints who sometimes sin. When a child of God sins, they are acting in a way that is not congruous with their true natures. It makes it much easier for us to default to sin when we think we are nothing more than sinners who have been saved by the grace of God.

We need to declare our new selves—who we have become in Christ. Let me give you an example. All international travelers are required to declare anything they purchased in whatever country they visited and are bringing back to this country. A declaration form is given to all passengers to declare what they are returning with. As children of God, what do we have to declare? Everything that Christ purchased for us by His life, death, and resurrection. Again, for most Christians, this will not be something that feels natural at first, but it will get easier as we practice it more.

When the enemy brings up your past *steps of stupid*, instead of allowing him to use manufactured evidence against you, start declaring the truth:

> For He made Him who knew no sin to be sin for us,
> that we might become the righteousness of God. (2
> Corinthians 5:21 NKJV)

Jesus was made what you were so you could be what He is. This is
your declaration as a child of God. Declare: I am the righteousness
of God! The more you openly declare who you are in Christ, the
freer you will be able to live your life. There is a saying that has been
around for a long time: When Satan brings up your past failures and
misdeeds to use against you, tell him that God has dropped all the
charges. Declare what the Word of God says about you—even if it
makes you feel weird and a little uneasy.

Knowing about God Is Not the Same as Knowing God

> One day Jesus said to a group of Jews who believed
> He was the Messiah; "If you *abide in My word*,
> you are My disciples indeed. And you shall *know
> the truth*, and *the truth shall make you free.*" (John
> 8:31–32 NKJV, emphasis added)

Jesus did not say that the truth sets you free. He said that when you
find your home in the Word of God, you will know the truth—and
the truth you know will set you free. Do you see why Jesus was able
to thwart the devil's attack on His identity by quoting the Word
(Luke 4:4–12 NKJV)? How can we defend ourselves adequately
when Satan attacks our identities if we do not know God's Word?
The Word of God is truth (John 17:17 NKJV).

Once we know His Word, we are in possession of truth. The
truth we know will set us free, and it will keep us free:

> Your word I have hidden in my heart, That I might
> not sin against You (Psalm 119:11 NKJV)

The psalmist did not say, "Your word I have filed away (memorized) in my head." It says, "Your word I have hidden (internalized) in my heart." Once again, we see how important it is to live our lives from the inside out.

Truth is not about having our heads full of biblical knowledge, facts, and memorized scriptures. Truth is not memorized facts about the Word of God that we regurgitate and quote. The devil does not care how much scripture you memorize and are able to quote—as long as you do not internalize it. When we internalize the Word, which is truth, a huge shift takes place. You no longer have the truth; the truth has you.

The devil has a hard time hustling a believer who knows who they are in Christ. The Word of God is the devil's nightmare. He hates the truth because he is a liar and the father of all lies. There is not one ounce of truth in him (John 8:44 NKJV). Truth will always expose the devil's shenanigans.

How We See Ourselves Will Depend on Where We Choose to Sit

Position, perception, and performance—these three things will be determined by you. Your position will determine your perception, and your perception will determine your performance. We could say it another way: "Where you choose to sit will determine how you see things. How you see things will determine how victorious you will be in living your life."

To illustrate this principle in a Sunday-morning service, I called two men to the front of our congregation. I placed a number on the floor. Each man chose a side to stand on. When I asked the men what they saw, one said, "I see a nine." The other one said, "I see a six." Those who were watching and listening heard the testimony of both men. Each man gave a different answer. How did they come to the conclusion about the number they saw on the floor? Their decisions were based on where the stood. Their positions determined what they saw. If we are to see ourselves as God sees us, then we need to see ourselves from His perspective; from where He sits.

> [And God] *raised us up together,* and *made us sit together in the heavenly places in Christ* Jesus. (Ephesians 2:6 NKJV, emphasis added)

We are here, but we are also there. How in the world can it be possible for us to be sitting here in the earthly realm and at the same time be seated in the heavenly realm? Since we are in Christ, we have to be where He is. It is impossible for the carnal mind to wrap itself around this spiritual truth.

As children of God, we are in two places—at the same time. Jesus is in us here in the physical realm, and we are in Him in the spiritual realm. He is in us here, and we are in Him there. This is weird thinking for most believers—even though it is clearly stated in the scriptures. This is outside of normal Christianity thinking. Our attention is so focused on who we were that we cannot see who we are. This has been said already, but it needs to be repeated. We are not physical beings who have spirits. We are spirits who live bodies. Our earthly bodies are temporary. Our spirits are eternal:

> Who then will condemn us? No one—for Christ Jesus died for us and was raised to life for us, and *he* (Jesus) *is sitting in the place of honor at God's right hand,* pleading for us. (Romans 8:34 NLT, emphasis added)

Where is Christ? Paul told us that He is sitting in heaven at the right hand of God. Keep this in mind as you read Romans 8:10:

> And *Christ lives within you,* so even though your body will die because of sin, the Spirit gives you life

because you have been made right with God. (NLT,
emphasis added)

We are in Christ, and Christ is in us. This simple nine-word sentence
tells it all.

One of my favorite scriptures in understanding my new self
identity is John 14:20. As you read this verse, pay close attention to
how it is constructed:

[Jesus said,] "At that day you will know that *I am
in My Father* and *you in Me*, and *I in you*." (NKJV,
emphasis added)

Jesus is in the Father, and we are in Jesus. If we are in Jesus, and He
is in the Father, then we are in the Father too. It gets even better.
Jesus said He is in us. Since Jesus is in the Father, and He is in us,
then the Father is also in us. Where is Jesus? He is in two places at
the same time. He is seated at the right hand of the Father in heaven,
and at the same time, He lives in us here on the earth.

Let me remind you one more time why we see things the way
we do. Our positions determine what we see. Are you beginning to
get it? As children of God, we have a choice that we did not have
before we had our born-from-above experience. We can choose
to see ourselves from our position in the natural realm (physical)
or from the advantage point of the spiritual realm. Since we are
spiritual beings who live in physical bodies, it is only possible for us
to know who we are when we see ourselves the way our Creator sees
us. Because our old lives were crucified with Christ and buried, He
only sees the new creations He made us to be—even when we are not
living up to our calling (Romans 6:6–12; Ephesians 4:1 NLT). How
we see ourselves determines what we believe, and what we believe
ultimately dictates how we live our lives. It really is that simple.

Most Christians struggle with their new identities in Christ
because they are so earthly minded that they are of no heavenly

good. The natural realm is more real to them than the eternal realm. This is understandable, but understanding is not the same thing as faith. The Bible clearly tells us what pleases God:

> And it is impossible to please God without faith. Anyone who wants to come to him must believe that God exists and that he rewards those who sincerely seek him. (Hebrews 11:6 NLT)

It is by faith that we accept the truth about our new creation identities—our new selves. The Word of God clearly tells us who we are. We should accept it without doubting or hesitating—even if our experiences are not presently jibing with what the Word of God says about our new selves. Faith pleases our heavenly Father.

What the community of faith needs more than anything is a reality check. If that is true, then what is reality? Simply stated, reality is whatever God says. It is not our experiences, feelings, or thoughts. Whatever God said was reality; whatever God says is reality; whatever God will say is reality. His Word will always be reality because it is the truth (John 17:17 NKJV).

When we step out of normal Christianity thinking, our focus will shift from the physical to the spiritual. In order to live up to our callings, we must shift our focus from the earthly realm to the heavenly realm where we are seated with Christ:

> Since you have been raised to *new life* with Christ, *set your sight on the realities of heaven*, where Christ sits in the place of honor at God's right hand. (Colossians 3:1 NLT, emphasis added)

The unseen realm (spiritual) is more real than the seen realm (physical).

Our Sin Record Has Been Expunged

Our sins were not covered by the blood of Jesus, like the blood of a sacrificial animal covered a person's sin under the Old Covenant, which had to be repeated over and over again because the blood of bulls and goats could not take away sin (Hebrews 10:4; 11 NKJV). It would take a perfect sacrifice and incorruptible blood for that to happen. Enter Jesus, the perfect Lamb of God. His blood removed our sins as far as the east is from the west (Psalm 103:12 NKJV):

> But this Man (Jesus), after *He had offered one sacrifice for sins forever*, sat down at the right hand of God. (Hebrews 10:12 NKJV, emphasis added)

Our sins of the past, present, and future were expunged from our records. When the truth of this revelation takes root deep down in your soul, your life will never be the same. Normal Christianity will no longer be appealing to you. Appearing to be weird or strange will not be on your radar. When you know your new creation self, the enemy will no longer be able to intimidate you.

"Nothing but the Blood" was written by Robert Lowry in 1876. This hymn is considered to be one of the patriotic anthems of the church:

> What can wash away my sin?
> Nothing but the blood of Jesus'
> What can make me whole again?
> Nothing but the blood of Jesus
> Refrain:
> Oh! precious is the flow
> That makes me white as snow;
> No other fount I know,
> Nothing but the blood of Jesus.

It is possible to sing the words of this great hymn and not actually believe the message that it communicates clearly and succinctly. If we really believed what we are singing, we would not be living the way we are living.

I saw the following statement recently, and I will admit that it put a burr under my saddle. I had to read it several times to make sure I was seeing it right. I do not think whoever said this meant to define the entire community of faith, but I am afraid it does for many:

> When the church became a nightclub, and the pulpit became a stage, the church became a carnal show to entertain the masses who are bored with spiritual things.

It is time for us to discover our new selves and who we are in Christ.

CHAPTER 8

THE ENEMY'S IED OF CHOICE

———

What we think about the most can either fuel us or fail us.
It has the power to shape our reality. Start thinking about
what you are thinking about, and adjust accordingly towards
the thoughts that lead you to happiness and hope.
—Robert Ricciardelli

There is a lot of wisdom in this statement. Start thinking about what you are thinking about. This is the first step in taking thoughts captive to the obedience of Christ (2 Corinthians 10:5 NKJV). If we do not take control of our thoughts, the day will come when they take control of us.

A thought cannot live unless it is spoken. Until then, it is just a thought. I encourage you to keep this in mind as you read this chapter. "Death and life are in the power of the tongue" (Proverbs 18:21 NKJV). The tongue can impart death or life. This is why it is so crucial to capture our thoughts and bring them in to line with the Word of God:

> *Bringing every thought into captivity* to the obedience
> of Christ. (2 Corinthians 10:5 NKJV, emphasis
> added)

Once we speak what we are thinking, we have given life to those thoughts—good or bad. The enemy we are fighting wants us to believe that since we thought it, we own it. Therefore, we might as well act on it. Do not allow the devil to sucker you with his deceit or live in your head rent-free.

Spiritual IEDs

An IED is an improvised explosive device that is designed to kill, mutilate, disfigure, or wound seriously. They are bombs constructed and deployed in ways other than in conventional military action. They are sometimes referred to as roadside bombs. These devices are so dangerous because you do not know they are there until detonation. The human carnage they cause can be devastating.

Satan has honed his skills in planting spiritual IEDs in the form of thoughts for millenniums. Since it worked so effectively in Genesis 3—on the first Adam—why change tactics. If it works, don't fix it. He planted a spiritual IED, cleverly disguised in the form of a thought, in Eve's mind: "Has God indeed said" (Genesis 3:1 NKJV). This thought metastasized until it exploded in full-blown disobedience. This thought that was planted between Adam's ears destroyed him, and it devastated the entire human race. Satan is very crafty in how he strategically uses thoughts to destroy, incapacitate, harass, distract, and wound Christians. The community of faith is filled with injured believers who have been taken out of action because of his spiritual IEDs.

Sometimes, if not most of the time, we are not even aware of the presence of these ticking time bombs until they blow. What detonates these IEDs are what I call *trigger moments*. A bad thought infiltrates our minds, left uncaptured, and then it festers until an event sets it off. When it is all said and done, we are shell-shocked by the way we acted or by what we said. Let me use myself as an example. You should be thankful that I am not going to use you to illustrate this truth!

Years ago, I had one of those neighbors who was not a happy camper—most of the time. You never knew what mood they were going to be in when you engaged them in a conversation. Occasionally, they were pleasant and cordial, but the majority of time they were *difficult*. One day, after a mild confrontation, a thought was planted between my ears: *I will get even someday*. Because I was so self-absorbed with my personal feelings, I failed to recognize the source of this thought and capture it; I owned it as mine. This uncaptured thought produced feelings, and the day came when I had the opportunity to act on these feelings. And did I redeem the time. Many Christians do not think this is a big deal. This is exactly what the serpent of Genesis 3:1 is gambling on. The enemy will make sure that a set up is forthcoming. You can take this to the bank—the enemy will make sure that we have the opportunity to act on what we think.

Sure enough, it happened. The day arrived. The IED the enemy had planted in my thought life would be detonated by a trigger event. I was blowing off the sidewalk after mowing my front yard, totally oblivious that my neighbor was in his truck backing up to where I was one hundred feet away. When he got alongside of me, he rolled down his window and began cursing at me. He told me in no uncertain terms that I better not blow my clippings in his yard—even though I was walking away from his house. That was the trigger event that detonated the IED the devil had planted in my head. Let me just say that it was not a very pleasant moment.

Did I tell you that I am a pastor? Pastors are not supposed to have moments like that. And wouldn't you know it? The next day was Sunday. To get free from what had transpired on Saturday, I came clean with my people. I told them the entire story—from the pulpit. To my utter amazement, they did not throw stones at me. The Holy Spirit taught us all a lesson that Sunday morning about the importance of capturing our thoughts, and I was released from my guilt. For the record, my neighbor and I have apologized for our behavior and are on speaking terms. I learned what I thought I knew: If you don't capture the thoughts that flow through your head, the day will come when those thoughts will capture you.

Here is the point I want to massage for a moment. The enemy of your soul is very sly. He knows that if he can get you to own the unhealthy thoughts he plants in your head, you will own them—and then he will make sure there is a trigger event that will activate them. I wonder how many marriages have been destroyed by thoughts that were given life by speaking them. Can you imagine how may friendships have been severed because of uncaptured thoughts? I can't fathom how many people have exited the community of faith because of thoughts that the enemy unobtrusively planted in their heads.

Be careful about the thoughts you choose to entertain. You could be hosting one of Satan's IEDs. If so, he will make sure you have the opportunity to act on it. Thoughts that are out of control will take control someday if they are not dealt with swiftly. We need to capture every thought that passes between our ears, holding onto what is good and rejecting what is not (2 Corinthian 10:5 NKJV).

The Mind Is a Battleground

The field of engagement with the enemy of our souls takes place six inches between our ears—in our heads. The importance of having a healthy thought life cannot be overstated. Trust me, if we continually lose the small skirmishes that takes place in our minds on a daily basis, it is just a matter of time before we succumb to the devil's wiles and are taken hostage.

What we know about thoughts—and how we respond to

them—will determine if we are victorious in this life or if we become victims:

> Stay alert! Watch out for *your great enemy, the devil.* He prowls around like a roaring lion, looking for someone to devour. (1 Peter 5:8 NLT, emphasis added)

If you find yourself continuously being eaten alive by your thought life, I suggest taking yourself off the menu. How? By learning to recognize the source of the unhealthy thoughts that infiltrate your mind and then capturing them.

I am convinced that most Christians have no idea that their biggest struggles take place in their thought lives. If you do not know where the battlefield is, it's hard to show up for battle. I promise you that the enemy knows where the battlefield is, and he will show up on time. It is impossible to win a war if you do not know where it is being fought. This is why we gave this book its subtitle: "Living Life from the Inside Out." It is a recipe for failure if we choose to engage in spiritual warfare from the outside in. That is flesh fighting flesh. That is one battle that will never be won by a child of God:

> *We use God's mighty weapons* (spiritual), not worldly (flesh) weapons, to knock down the strongholds of human reasoning (mind) and to destroy false arguments. (2 Corinthians 10:4 NLT, emphasis added)

It does not get any clearer than that. The battlefield is in our minds, and the weapons we have to fight and win with are spiritual in nature.

Why has Satan chosen our minds as the battleground for spiritual warfare? Because our minds are our greatest assets. He knows that whatever gets your mind gets you. He also hates being exposed. Satan does not like it when things are brought out into the open. He does his best work in secret, undercover. The spiritual battle that all Christians are involuntarily engaged in, knowingly or unknowingly, takes place in an invisible realm—between the ears. It is possible to know what a person believes by their behavior, but it is impossible to see what goes on in a person's mind:

> The thief (devil) does not come except to *steal*, and to *kill*, and to *destroy*. (John 10:10 NKJV, emphasis added)

The thief has the ability to convince us that all the unhealthy and ungodly thoughts that pop into our heads belong to us. Because we have lived with thoughts going in and out of our heads for a long time, it is easy for him to disguise his thoughts as our own. If we take ownership of those thoughts, he has accomplished his mission. We will destroy, incapacitate, and wound ourselves without his assistance. Spiritual warfare begins in our minds, and it will end in our minds—win or lose. This is why the Word of God tells us to capture every thought and bring it into captivity.

The mind is the battlefield. The battle rages in our heads every day—from small skirmishes to full-blown engagements.

Clearing, Cleaning, and Cleansing the Battlefield

I only had three baths during my tour in Vietnam in 1968. That is not a typo. Three! To add to our misery, we were not allowed to use deodorant or cologne. We spent our time in the jungle and could not risk being sniffed out by the enemy. No pun intended. We did smell, but we blended in very nicely with the jungle.

I took my first bath in the South China Sea. That was one horrendous mistake on my part. We looked like walking salt blocks once we got out of the water and dried off. The 110-degree temperature did not help matters. We were more miserable after our brief swim than we had been before we entered the water. You have not lived until you spend thirty days in a steaming hot jungle galled by salt water. It makes you a little irritable.

My second bath was taken in a muddy, stinky river. We cast all caution to the wind and dove in because we were so hot. We did not get clean, but we did pick up a lot of unwelcomed hitchhikers—leeches. The leeches removed more from our tired, dirty bodies than the murky water in the river did. My third time to bathe was at a fire support base. We were all given an allotted three-minute shower. Yep, a whopping three minutes. It may have been the fastest three minutes of my life. I cannot tell you how good that short shower felt.

When I talk about clearing, cleaning, and cleansing the battlefield, I am not talking about bathing in water—even though I am a proponent of good hygiene. The sacred territory between our ears is what I am talking about. The mind is the battlefield. Spiritual battles are fought there. Our thought lives—the sacred areas where we think, feel, reason, and will—are what needs attention. God has provided the resource for that (His Word):

> For husbands, this means love your wives, just as Christ loved the church. He gave up his life for her to make her holy and clean, *washed by the cleansing of God's Word*. (Ephesians 5:25–26 NLT, emphasis added)

What water is capable of doing on the outside, the Word of God does on the inside. The Word of God has the power to clear our minds of Satan's strategically placed thoughts—his IEDs of choice.

I love what Chuck Swindoll said about being washed by the Word:

> The word washes us deep down inside our souls. It purifies our thoughts, scrubs our motives, and

cleans our conscious as we soak in it and obey its truths.

We defend and protect ourselves with the Word of God. When the devil tries to infiltrate our thought lives with the intention of perverting our thinking, we need to take our stand on God's Word. The enemy has no defense against the power of the Word of God:

> Don't worry about anything; instead, pray about everything. Tell God what you need, and thank him for all the has done. Then you will experience *God's peace*, which exceeds anything we can understand. *His peace will guard your hearts and minds* as you live in Christ Jesus. (Philippians 4:6–7 NLT, emphasis added)

The next time the enemy tries to sucker-punch you with unhealthy thoughts, hoping you will buy into the lie they are yours, start thanking God for all He has done for you. Turn your thoughts to Him, and His peace will stand guard over your thoughts and feelings. You are at *peace with God* because you have been born from above (Romans 5:1 NKJV). This gives you access to the *peace of God* that is available to all of His children.

Exposing the Enemy's Motives

The devil hates God. You need to put that information in a permanent file inside your head. Make no mistake about it—the devil does not like us either. He knows how much God loves His children, and it infuriates him. He hates what God loves because he hates God. He knows we are the apple of God's eyes, and he does his best to plant worms in God's apples by sowing unhealthy thoughts. This battle is not about who we are; it is about who we belong to. The devil gets great pleasure out of hurting what God loves the most.

In Genesis 3, we see that the plot of the enemy was to totally eviscerate God's creation: humanity. The only way this overthrow could succeed was if he could get humanity to rebel against their Creator. He did this by planting a seed of doubt in the minds of Adam and Eve about the trustworthiness of God: "Did God really say?" (Genesis 3:1 NLT). In other words, can you really trust God and what He says? These words do not sound that threatening. If we believe that, we are giving the enemy a toehold to do greater damage. This is why the Word of God tells us to bring *every thought* into captivity. Once thoughts are captured, we can sift through them, exposing the ones that are not from God and those that have been subtly planted by the hater of God. In the midst of perfection, Adam and Eve did not recognize what the serpent was doing. He was sowing thoughts that had the power to determine destiny.

Let's wade out in the waters of the Word all the way back to the book of Genesis and see if we can expose the enemy's motives for choosing the mind as the battlefield to engage us in spiritual warfare. What did God tell Adam?

> And the Lord God commanded the man, *saying,* "Of every tree of the garden you may freely eat; but of the tree of the knowledge of good and evil *you shall not eat,* for in the day that you eat of it you shall surely die." (Genesis 2:16 NKJV, emphasis added)

God was not ambiguous in any way, shape, or form when He told Adam what he could eat and not eat. You may eat freely from any tree in the garden—except from the tree of the knowledge of good and evil. The fruit from this tree is not on your menu. Leave it alone. It will cost you your life if you disobey.

The first thing the serpent did was plant a seed of doubt in the mind of Adam and Eve about what God said: "Did God really say?"

We just read what Adam heard God say about not eating from the forbidden tree. Because Adam and Eve did not capture this thought and examine it under the microscope of God's Word, they exposed themselves to greater deception. Eve should have said, "God told us not to eat the fruit from that tree. Case closed." By not taking thoughts captive that drift through our minds, we give the enemy an opportunity to plant an IED, and all it needs is a trigger event to set it off.

Eve repeated what God told them to the serpent about eating from the forbidden tree. The consequences of disobedience would be sure death. To this, the serpent said: "You will not surely die" (Genesis 3:4 NKJV). He goes from crafting the Word of God—"Did God really say?"—to contradicting what God said: "You will not die."

Thoughts that contradict the Word of God are not coming from you. Satan's ploy is to get you to own his thoughts as your own. He wants you to be suspicious of the credibility of what God says. If he succeeds, he gains more control of the battlefield. He cannot have what we do not give him. If we give the devil an inch, he will take a mile. The enemy will be able to take advantage of us in bigger ways later if we continually lose small skirmishes. He will demand more and more. As I said earlier, if we do not take thoughts captive, they will capture us at some point in time.

If the devil ever seizes control of the narrative, it is only a matter of time before he is able to defeat a child of God on the battlefield of their mind. His method of operation is to craft his own version of the truth, contradicting the truth, and conceal the truth:

> Then the serpent said to the woman, "You will not surely die. For God knows that in the day you eat of it your eyes will be opened, and you will be like God, knowing good and evil." (Genesis 3:4–5 NKJV)

The serpent cunningly conceals two truths. The first one was an attack on their identities: "You will be like God." However, they were already like God. Disobeying God would rob them of their identities. "The thief does not come except to steal, and to kill, and to destroy" (John 10:10 NKJV). He is very good at concealing the truth.

The second truth the enemy concealed was the consequences of disobeying God. He did not say a word about being kicked out of heaven for his disobedience (Isaiah 14:12–17 NKJV). The devil knew that if he could get them to disobey God, they would be removed from the Garden of Eden—just as he had been removed from heaven. All of this began with one small thought that was planted: "Did God really say?" (Genesis 3:1 NLT).

Satan has chosen our minds as the battleground for spiritual warfare engagement because he knows that if he can plant thoughts that are contrary to what God says, they will metastasize, which will bring sure destruction and defeat for a child of God. Capturing thoughts is not an option; it is tantamount to living a victorious life. When we throw the Word of God, which is truth, in the face of the enemy, he has no defense against it. He knows that, but he sure hopes you never do.

Winning Daily Skirmishes in Our Minds

A key component to winning battles that take place in our heads every day is knowing our enemy:

> Stay alert! Watch out for *your great enemy, the devil.* He prowls around like a roaring lion, looking for someone to devour. (2 Peter 5:8 NLT, emphasis added)

The greatest foe we have is the one we do not know we have. It amazes me that the majority of Christians have no idea who they are at war with. Many do not even know they are in a war. I was in that category for the majority of my life. Before the Spirit of God woke me up to the truth, I believed the unhealthy thoughts I had were my own. I did everything in my power to overcome them: I prayed more, read more, worked harder, ad infinitum. The only thing I accomplished was wearing myself out and wrestling with guilt. This is exactly what the enemy of your soul wants you to do (Daniel 7:25 NKJV).

Paul wrote these words in his second letter to the church in Corinth:

> But I fear, lest somehow as the serpent deceived Eve by his craftiness, so your minds may be corrupted from the simplicity that is in Christ. (2 Corinthians 11:3 NKJV)

If the devil can control your mind, he will be able to control your life. The serpent was able to control the lives of Adam and Eve because he was able to corrupt their thoughts. The opposite is true as well. If we allow the Spirit of God to control our minds, our lives will be under His control.

What we choose to set our minds on will determine if we overcome Satan's IEDs or become statistics. It is our choice:

> For those who live according to the flesh set their minds (thoughts) on the things of the flesh, but those who live according to the Spirit, the things (thoughts) of the Spirit. For to be carnally (flesh) minded is death, but to be spiritually minded is life and peace. Because the carnal mind (flesh) is enmity against God; for it is not subject to the law of God, nor indeed can be. So then, those who are in the flesh cannot please God. *But you are not in the flesh but in the Spirit,* if indeed the Spirit of God dwells in you. Now if anyone does not have

the Spirit of Christ, he is not His. (Romans 8:5–9
NKJV, emphasis added)

Are you saved? Have you accepted Jesus Christ as your Lord and
Savior? Have you had an encounter with Christ that has radically
transformed your life? If so, you are no longer in the flesh. You are
in the Spirit, which gives you the ability to capture every thought
that sneaks into your head and replace lies with the truth of God:

But we understand these things, for we have the
mind of Christ. (1 Corinthians 2:16 NLT)

CHAPTER 9

ARRAYED FOR BATTLE

P eople who know me well will tell you that I am not a movie buff. I cannot tell you the names of recent movies or present-day actors and actresses. And it is not because I am opposed to movies. It is not something I get pleasure from. I have other things to do rather to sit for a couple of hours watching a movie. I extend kudos to those who can. I can't.

With that said, I have to admit that there are a couple of thirty-minute TV western shows that I watch regularly. It is not uncommon for my wife to say, "It's about time for your *Gunsmoke* to come on." Did you notice what she said? *My Gunsmoke*. I wonder what she means by that. When it was about time for my *Gunsmoke* to come on, she once had the unmitigated gall to say, "I would bet you have seen every episode at least fifty times." Now, my wife has the tendency to exaggerate a little. I would wager that I have not seen every episode more than forty-five times—but certainly not fifty.

In some of the episodes, Marshal Matt Dillon (James Arness) finds himself in some precarious situations. There have been times when this United States Marshal of Dodge City, Kansas, looked like he was about to meet his waterloo. Somehow, he found a way out. He escaped just in time so he could be in the next episode. Amazing!

I was watching an episode where Marshall Dillon had gotten himself in a pickle. Things were not looking good for my hero. My stomach was in a knot, my pulse rate had increased, and I found myself sitting on the edge of my chair with both hands clutched together. All of a sudden, the light of reality turned on. I had seen this particular episode forty-five times (not fifty), and everything turns out okay. My hero wins!

With that awareness, I sat back in my chair, relaxed, and enjoyed the ending. Everything turned out exactly how I had seen it before. As Yogi Berra said, "It's déjà vu all over again." Why was I in such an emotional state when I knew how it was going to turn out? When you have seen the movie before, you know how it will end. The good guy wins. The bad guy loses. When we know how things are going to turn out in life, it helps us to keep standing when we are struggling to stay upright. God has shown us how life on earth is going to end. This really helps when it looks like the enemy may knock you off your feet, when you feel like your situation is hopeless, or when you are contemplating hoisting the white flag of surrender. Keep reminding yourself that the Lord has shown you how this is going to end.

God Has Already Scripted the Ending

As long as we are living in this physical world, we will have struggles (John 16:33 NKJV). It is not *if* we find ourselves in spiritual warfare; it is *when*. Sometimes it will be small conflicts, and at other times, it will be a full-blown engagement with the enemy of our souls. Sometimes the spiritual fights we find ourselves in are just nagging irritations that pass fairly quickly. Sometimes the fight is so severe that we are not sure survival is possible.

Jesus gave us a heads-up about the spiritual conflict we will face while living on this side of eternity:

> *I have told you* all this so that *you may have peace in me.* Here *on earth you will have many trials and sorrows.* But take heart, because *I have overcome the world.* (John 16:33 NLT, emphasis added)

Our peace is always found in Christ when we find ourselves in confrontations with the enemy of fear. When you are engaged in spiritual warfare, keep reminding yourself of what the Word of God says:

> *The God of peace will soon crush Satan under your feet.* May the grace of our Lord Jesus be with you. (Romans 16:20 NLT, emphasis added)

Don't you just love that? The God of peace will soon crush Satan under *our feet.* In case you are wondering how things will turn out for believers in this real-life movie, I will ruin the ending for you—we win.

> But thanks be to God, who gives us the victory through our Lord Jesus Christ. (1 Corinthians 15:57 NKJV)

Knowing that we win in this life—and in the afterlife too—should encourage us to fight our spiritual battles fearlessly, knowing the outcome has already been scripted by God. When the battle intensifies, don't lose heart. Instead, stand your ground (Ephesians 6:14 NLT).

Spiritual Warfare Begins and Ends in Our Heads

As children of God, we have home-field advantage. Most sports teams play a little harder when the game is played before their home crowd. Playing in your own house stimulates you emotionally and activates the adrenal glands to pump more adrenaline, which empowers you physically. Playing before an enthusiastic audience that is cheering you on makes you play harder, which gives you an advantage over your opponent. Sometimes this is referred to as playing "over your head." That simply means that your environment creates an atmosphere that causes you to play beyond your capabilities:

> For I can do everything through Christ, who gives
> me strength. (Philippians 4:13 NLT)

Most teams win more games at home than they do in away games.

The enemy of our souls has chosen our minds as the battlefields of engagement. Since they are our minds, we have home-field advantage. He's in our house now—illegally. God has given us the authority and power to evict him. The enemy knows this. This is why he tries so hard to disguise unhealthy thoughts as being ours. He wants us to own them. If he is successful, there is a chance that we will eventually act on them, sometimes resulting in devastating consequences. This is the clever ruse he used on Eve in Genesis to get her to disobey God. Since this tactic was an overwhelming success, he has not deviated from this stratagem.

The spiritual battle that we believers are having is taking place on our home turf, and we are fighting like we are in an away game. The stands are packed with believers who are cheering us on:

> Therefore, since we are *surrounded by such a huge*
> *crowd* of witnesses to the life of faith, let us strip
> off every weight that slows us down, especially *the*
> *sin* (unbelief) that so easily trips us up. And let us

run with endurance the race God has set before us"
(Hebrews 12:1 NLT, emphasis added)

This great crowd of witnesses is listed in Hebrews 11. When we catch a hold of this truth, spiritual adrenaline (the Holy Spirit) will empower us to fight like we have never fought before. The enemy does not have a chance when the children of God know their new creation identities in Christ. Satan cannot win because he is fighting God. We know how that turned out at Calvary's cross, don't we? And so do the devil and his cohorts. It is impossible to win a war if you do not show up on the right battlefield or know the tactics of your enemy.

The most lethal weapon the enemy has are thoughts that he secretly plants in our minds. They are camouflaged as our thoughts. This is why the Word of God tells us to capture every thought that passes through our heads. This might be a good time to reread chapter 1. Our battles come from within. If we are going to mature in our new creation identities—who we have been made in Christ—we must win the skirmishes that take place in our thought lives on a daily basis. It begins in our heads, it affects our hearts, and then it manifests through our feet. What we give power to has power over us—if we allow it.

Exposing the Devil's Battle Strategy

Back in the 1970s, I read a statement that has stuck with me like wet West Texas caliche. "You don't invent truth, truth is discovered." What is truth? Jesus gives us the answer to that question in the Gospel of John:

> Make them holy by *your truth*; teach them *your word, which is truth.* (John 17;17 NLT, emphasis added)

When we discover what the Word of God says about anything, we are in possession of the greatest weapon that has ever been or will ever be: truth. This is why the enemy reacts to truth so savagely. Anytime you hear a person respond to truth (the word of God) as being hate speech, you are getting a glimpse of Satan's influence in that person's thought life about new creation identity. Truth does sound like hate to those who hate truth. No one hates truth more than the devil:

> For you are the children of your father the devil, and you love to do the evil things he does. He was a murderer from the beginning. *He has always hated the truth*, because *there is no truth in him*. When he lies, it is consistent with his character; for *he is a liar and the father of lies*. (John 8:44 NLT, emphasis added)

Truth eviscerates all demonic forces that want to take us out. This is why it is imperative that we, as children of God, discover the truth about our new creation identities. The devil will fight tooth and nail in his attempt to keep his weakness from being exposed and your strength from being revealed. This will make more sense when we talk about the sword of the Spirit in chapter 10.

One of the most familiar passages of scripture concerning spiritual warfare is found in the book of Ephesians when Paul talks about the armor of God.

> Put on the *whole armor of God*, that you may be able to stand against the wiles of the devil. (Ephesians 6:11 NKJV, emphasis added)

Since we are engaged in a spiritual war, it is imperative that we are fully dressed for the fray. For far too long, the community of faith has been filled with "spiritual streakers." Our tendency is to pick and choose which piece of armor we want to wear, but the instructions are to put on the full armor of God. Notice whose armor it is. Here is some inside information: God's armor is custom-fit for every soldier (2 Timothy 2:3–4 NKJV).

Why does it have to be God's armor? Can't we face off with the enemy while wearing our own armor? If we try to fight spiritual battles with physical weapons, we will end up as casualties. Our battle is not with flesh and blood:

> For *we do not wrestle against flesh and blood*, but against principalities, against powers, against the rulers of the darkness of this age against spiritual hosts of wickedness in the heavenly places. (Ephesians 6:12 NKJV, emphasis added)

The battle does not take place in the seen realm. The war is fought in our minds—in the unseen realm. This is why the full armor of God is required.

Paul uses the word *wrestle* in this Ephesian passage. This word is used figuratively to describe the spiritual conflict we are in. He could have used the word *box*, but you can box from a distance. Wrestling, on the other hand, is done up close and personal. The enemy is constantly grappling with and striving to trip us, throw us down, or knock us off balance. This is why Paul repeatedly tells us to stand firm and stand our ground.

If we are going to be successful in winning this wrestling match, we need to know our opponent's strengths and weaknesses. Our wrestling coach, Paul, tells us to stand against the wiles of the devil and know his cunning stratagems. The better you know your opponent, the easier it is to defeat him (1 Peter 5:8 NKJV).

What are the wiles of the devil? Sometimes this word is translated as *schemes*, and at other times, it is translated as *strategies*. The Greek word for *wile* is *methodia*. In English, it would be *methods*. How can we stand against the wiles of the devil if we do not know his methods or schemes? There has always been a need to know what the battle plans of the enemy are, but it is even more important today. I am afraid that most Christians have no idea. The misconception many believers have is this: "If I leave the devil alone, he will leave me alone." This is deception, and it is dangerous. Let me give you some insight into deception. Deception is dangerous because it is deceiving. When it comes to spiritual warfare, ignorance is not bliss. Not knowing can cost you everything.

By connecting Ephesians 6:11 with 2 Corinthians 2, we will define the wiles of the devil. What is his strategy? In his first letter to the church in Corinth, Paul addresses an immoral issue that was present in the congregation. Everyone knew about it, but no one did anything to resolve it. The people, including the leadership, expressed no sorrow or shame about it (1 Corinthian 5:1–5 NKJV). Paul's counsel to the church was to remove this individual from the fellowship until they repented. The church did what Paul advised them to do. Evidently, this person did repent and was received back into the fold. In his second letter, Paul commends them for restoring this individual:

> I wrote to you as I did to test you and see if you would fully comply with my instructions. When you forgive this man, I forgive him, too. And when I forgive whatever needs to be forgiven, I do so with Christ's authority for your benefit, so that Satan will not outsmart us. For we are familiar with his *evil schemes.* (2 Corinthians 2:9–11 NLT, emphasis added)

Here, we find the word *schemes* again. Satan can take advantage of us if we do not know his devious battle plan. The word *scheme* used in 2 Corinthians 2:11 is not the same word used in Ephesians 6:11. This Greek word is *noema*, which denotes *thought*. Aha! Are you beginning to get the picture?

The devil's scheme is to turn our thought lives into "mind-fields."

His strategy is to infiltrate our thought lives and sow his thoughts, hoping we will own them as our own. If we take possession of the enemy's thoughts, the chances of us acting on them increases immeasurably. This is why the Word of God tells us to capture every rebellious thought and bring it into captivity to the obedience of Christ (2 Corinthians 10:5 NLT). Capturing thoughts can be a matter of life and death.

Spiritual Armor

Ephesians is one of the four prison epistles written by Paul. The other three are Philippians, Colossians, and Philemon. They are called *prison epistles* because they were written from the confines of a prison cell. We would never have known Paul was incarcerated when he wrote these letters if he had not told us. His circumstances never determined his peace. His peace determined how he dealt with his circumstances. Christ was his peace.

Paul spent a lot of time chained to soldiers who were given the responsibility of standing guard over him. Can you imagine what it must have been like to be tethered to Paul for an extended period of time. I am sure every soldier who had this assignment got an earful of Jesus. Instead of bemoaning his plight, Paul seized the moment and used the armor that the Roman soldiers were wearing as an analogy for the spiritual armor that God has made available for all of his children:

> *Put on all of God's armor* so that *you will be able to stand firm* against *all strategies* of the devil. (Ephesians 6:11 NLT, emphasis added)

Paul says it again two verses later:

> Therefore, *put on every piece of God's armor* so you will be able to resist (withstand) the enemy in the time of evil. (Ephesians 6:13 NLT, emphasis added)

There are three things that scream for attention in these two verses. The first one is that we are to put on *all* of God's armor. The spiritual battle that we are engaged in on a daily basis requires the full armor of God. It is a sure recipe for defeat if we omit any piece. The second thing we need to pay attention to is that the armor we are told to put on belongs to God. It is God's armor. God sees what we cannot see. God knows what we do not know. He is able to see how everything ends because it has already been scripted.

The enemy we are fighting knows how things will turn out too, and it will not be good for him. Between now and then, there will be a battle. We are told to put on the full armor of God so we will be adequately armed against the attacks of the enemy. The third thing that is worth noting is that the armor of God will empower us to stand against all of the strategies and weapons the devil has in his arsenal. How good is that. The devil has no strategy or battle plan that will ever be successful against a well-informed, well-equipped child of God. He knows that too. Let me remind you of something you may have forgotten. God will not tell us to do something that was impossible for us to do. Therefore, we can put on His custom-fit spiritual armor, engage the enemy on the battlefield, and—here's the exciting part—win every time.

There are six pieces of armor mentioned in Ephesians 6. Five are for defensive purposes (protection), and one is primarily for offense. In this chapter, I will briefly cover the five defensive pieces of armor. The focus of the following chapter will be solely on the sword of the Spirit, which is the Word of God. Try to picture in your mind what a Roman soldier would be wearing as he was chained to Paul. Paul used the soldier's physical armor as an analogy for the spiritual armor every Christian has at their disposal when they find themselves engaged in spiritual warfare.

The Belt of Truth

> Gird your waist with truth. (Ephesians 6:14 NKJV)

The first piece of armor we are told to put on is the belt of truth. Why begin with the belt of truth? The belt of truth fastens every weapon in its proper place. It would be disastrous for a warrior to enter battle without a strong belt to keep every weapon in a ready position, making them easily accessible to his hands. This is why the belt is the first thing a soldier puts on.

The foe we face on a daily basis may be formidable, but he is helpless against truth. Jesus called Satan a liar and said that he is void of all truth (John 8:44 NKJV). Truth is his kryptonite. Truth rats him out every time. His lies have no penetrating power against the Word of God. Jesus said that even the gates of Hades (hell) have no defense against the truth (Matthew 16:13–19 NKJV). Truth never changes—no matter what strategy the enemy uses in his attempt to take us out. It enables us to keep standing in the midst of spiritual conflict when others are falling. Everything rises or falls on truth. The truth is not what we make it; good and bad are relative. Truth is whatever God says about anything; therefore, it is absolute.

Jesus said that He was the way and *the truth* (John 14:6 NKJV). This is why the first piece of armor we are to put on is the belt of truth.

The Breastplate of Righteousness

> Put on the breastplate of righteousness. (Ephesians 6:14 NKJV)

The breastplate that a soldier wore protected his heart and other vital organs from the waist up, and it was secured by the belt. It would be suicidal for a Roman soldier to engage in hand-to-hand combat without protecting the most vital area of his body. Without the breastplate, a soldier could suffer a strike that would result in instant death. Knowing they were properly protected gave them added courage and confidence when they engaged their enemy.

For a child of God, it is not just a breastplate. It is the breastplate of *righteousness*. This word was formerly spelled *"rightwiseness."* Righteousness is an incredible gift that God gives to those who believe in and accept Jesus Christ as their Lord and Savior. They are brought into right standing with God, which they could never obtain on their own. A person becomes in Christ all that God requires for them to be, which they could never be in themselves.

Whenever we find ourselves in the middle of spiritual conflict, the enemy will do anything and everything to penetrate our most vulnerable areas—our spiritually vital organs—primarily the heart and then the lungs and other organs necessary for life. God's breastplate of righteousness prevents Satan from being able to deliver a fatal blow. Since the armor belongs to God, the enemy must get through Him to get to us. That is not going to happen.

Adam Clark's Commentary says, "As the breastplate defends the heart and lungs, and all those vital functionaries that are contained in what is called the region of the thorax; so, this righteousness defends everything on which the man's spiritual existence depends."

Without it, we stand alone. With it, we stand in God (Isaiah 59:17 NKJV).

Shoes of Peace

> Having shod your feet with the preparation of the
> gospel of peace. (Ephesians 6:15 NKJV)

The importance of being able to stand firmly when we are in a fight cannot be overstated. In the midst of battle, being properly shod is crucial for being victorious or becoming a statistic. A soldier could not risk slipping or falling in battle because they did not have the right shoes on their feet. Can you imagine a soldier going into battle in a pair of flip-flops or Crocs? What would that say about that particular soldier? Do you think the enemy would not notice what he had on his feet? The enemy would be emboldened because he would know his combatant's footing was not stable.

The intensity of the spiritual battle we are constantly being lured into demands that we have a solid foundation under us. The only adequate support is the Gospel of peace. Peace is what determines fight or flight. The word *preparation* denotes readiness and being prepared. This preparedness empowers you to stand when everything in you is screaming for you to run. You are able to hold your ground when others are fleeing because you are in right standing with God. Christ is your peace (Ephesians 2:14 NKJV).

No matter how fierce the battle may be, do not retreat. Stand and fight. You have a firm foundation under you—shoes of peace. The *peace of God* will guard our hearts and minds (our thoughts and emotions) because we are at *peace with God* (Philippians 4:7; Romans 5:1 NKJV).

Shield of Faith

> Above all, taking *the shield of faith* with which you will be able to quench *all the fiery darts* of the wicked one. (Ephesians 6:16 NKJV, emphasis added)

The shield of faith is the fourth piece of armor that Paul mentions. A soldier's shield gave him the advantage to intercept specific attacks from close-range weapons like swords, knives, stones, and the like. This is why Paul said, "Above all, take the shield of faith." A Roman soldier's shield was not a small piece of armor. It was usually as large as a door, giving him the advantage of covering his entire body. Oftentimes, soldiers would interlock their shields to create an impenetrable barrier around themselves. This was done mostly when the enemy was launching fiery arrows or darts. This strategy of joining their shields together strengthened and fortified them. It gave the soldiers confidence.

When we are strong in faith, it makes it impossible for the enemy to break through and land a blow. Faith convinces us that God will do what He promised. When we fight in faith, we can be certain that God will be true to His Word. Faith forms that protective barrier between us and the schemes of the devil. Faith keeps us grounded in truth, exposes the lies of the enemy, and guarantees a victorious outcome.

Helmet of Salvation

> And take the helmet of salvation. (Ephesians 6:17 NKJV)

A Roman soldier wore a helmet to protect his head from receiving a blow that could lead to instant death. A good protective helmet was vital to his survival. If the head was severely wounded, the rest of the armor would be of little value.

Since the mind is the battlefield where spiritual warfare is carried out, it is imperative that we have our heads protected at all times. When we are confident of our union with Christ, our minds are protected from discouragement and the desire to flee when things seem to be falling apart. The assurance of salvation is our impenetrable defense against anything the enemy may throw at us.

The more we understand how important the helmet of salvation is for our daily survival, the more insulated we become to the enemy's subtle infiltration into our thought lives. He wants to influence our thinking. Confidence in our salvation exposes the traps he sets to ensnare us.

Our thought lives must be protected at all costs. It is the choke point that leads to victory or defeat:

> These things I have written to you who believe in the name of the Son of God, *that you may know* that you have eternal life, and that you may continue to believe in the name of the Son of God. (1 John 5:13 NKJV, emphasis added)

We must never underestimate the need because knowing it is well with our souls. Salvation is so much more than future benefits in the sweet by-and-by. Salvation is also for the nasty now and now:

> *Put on the whole armor of God*, that you may be *able to stand* against the wiles of the devil. (Ephesians 6:11 NKJV, emphasis added)

The full armor of God is available to every believer. Whatever you do, don't be a spiritual streaker! As a child of God, you have been destined to reign in this life through Jesus Christ (Romans 5:17 NKJV).

Many Christians are not dressed for war because they do not know they are in a war. Is there any wonder the casualty rate is so high within the community of faith?

CHAPTER 10

THE SWORD OF THE SPIRIT

———

O f the six pieces of armor mentioned in Ephesians 6, the sword of the Spirit is the only one that is primarily used as an offensive weapon. Paul leaves us with no doubt about what the sword of the Spirit is. The sword of the Spirit is the Word of God (Ephesians 6:17 NKJV). The enemy is out to destroy God's people but has absolutely no defense against God's Word. Think about how *sword* is spelled: s-word. Sword is the "Spirit word or, as Paul said, "the sword of the Spirit." The Word of God is a sword, and it has the ability and power to cut through anything the enemy may raise up against us in his attempt to take us out.

The S Word

Let's go back to the beginning of time and listen to a conversation God had with Himself:

> Then God said, *"Let Us* make man *in Our image,*
> according to *Our likeness."* (Genesis 1:26 NKJV,
> emphasis added)

Let us? Here is an obvious question that begs to be answered: Who is God talking to when He said, that? Our image? Our likeness? To find the answer to this question, let's jump over millennia and into the Gospel of John:

> In the beginning was *the Word,* and *the Word* was
> with God, and *the Word* was God. *He* (the Word)
> was in the beginning with God. All things were
> made through Him (the Word), and without Him
> (the Word) nothing was made that was made. In
> Him (the Word) was life, and the life was the light
> of men. And the light shines in the darkness, and
> the darkness did not comprehend it. (John 1:1–5
> NKJV, emphasis added)

I encourage you to reread those five verses one more time because John tells us exactly who Jesus is. The Word was with God when time was started, and the Word was God. Without the Word, nothing would have been made because everything was made through the Word. Now we know Who God was talking to when He was bringing all of creation into existence. He was talking to Himself! In case you think that God talking to Himself is weird or strange, pay close attention the next time you carry on a conversation with yourself. We talk to ourselves all the time.

The story of the sword of the Spirit continues:

> So *the Word became human* and made *his* home
> among us. *He* was full of unfailing love and
> faithfulness. And we have seen his glory, the glory

of *the Father's one and only Son.* (John 1:14 NLT, emphasis added)

The Word in the beginning of time was Jesus Christ, the Son of God. This is why Jesus told Philip, "He who has seen Me has seen the Father" (John 14:9 NKJV). To know Jesus is to know the Father because they are One. This sheds a lot of light on a passage found in 1 John:

> Whoever denies the Son does not have the Father either; he who acknowledges the Son has the Father also. (1 John 2:23 NKJV)

When the right time came, God wrapped Himself up in human flesh and entered the natural realm. The Word became human. Both Matthew and Luke give an account of this moment:

> Now after Jesus (the Word) was born in Bethlehem of Judea in the days of Herod the king, behold, wise men from the East came to Jerusalem, saying, "Where is He who has been born King of the Jews? For we have seen His star in the East and have come to worship Him." (Matthew 2:1–2 NKJV, emphasis added)

Born a king? No one is born a king. One may be born a prince and later become a king, but no one is born a king. This was the first time it happened, and it will never happen again.

Luke says this about Jesus's birth:

> And she (Mary) brought forth her firstborn Son (the Word), and wrapped Him (the Word) in swaddling clothes, and laid Him (the Word) in a manger;

because there was no room for them in the end.
(Luke 2:7 NKJV, emphasis added)

In an obscure Bethlehem stable, a manger is filled with God—the Word incarnate:

And the Word (Jesus) became flesh and dwelt among us, and we beheld His (the Word) glory, the glory as of the only begotten of the Father, full of grace and truth" (John 1:14 NKJV, emphasis added)

The Word, the One who created the world in Genesis 1, is now in the world He created—as King.

This born King is called Jesus Christ. His name reveals His identity. The name Jesus addresses His humanity. He was the Child born of Mary (Isaiah 9:6 NKJV). The name Christ addresses His divinity. He was the Son sent by the Father (Galatians 4:4 NKJV). We can define the incarnation as divinity living in humanity. The Word became human. This is why Jesus said, "If you had known Me, you would have known My Father also; and from now on you know Him (the Father) and have seen Him" (John 14:7 NKJV, emphasis added).

Those words deal with the deity of Jesus better than any commentary you can buy. Jesus told Philip that when you look at Me, you are seeing God because we are One and the same. Jesus is God expressing Himself through the Word.

The Power and Purpose of the Written Word

For the Word of God is alive and powerful. It is sharper than the sharpest two-edged sword, cutting between soul and spirit, between joint and marrow.

It exposes our innermost thoughts and desires. (Hebrews 4:12 NLT)

The first thing the writer of Hebrews says about the written Word of God is that it is powerful. It is so effective and efficient that the enemy has no way to parry it. When the sword of the Spirit is wielded, the enemy has no defense against it—and he must flee.

The written Word of God is sharper than the sharpest two-edged sword. No physical sword can compete with the sword of the Spirit. Every child of God is in a spiritual battle, but it is not a physical confrontation. If we try to fight a spiritual battle with the sharpest two-edge sword, we will become casualties. This is why we are to take up spiritual armor, which includes the offensive weapon called the sword of the Spirit.

The written Word of God has the capability to do what a surgeon's scalpel is incapable of doing. It can separate the soul from the spirit. The Word of God is so powerful, so precise, and so sharp that it can divide things that appear to be indivisible. The written Word also has the power to expose and discern our innermost thoughts and desires, which a surgeon's light could never do.

A shift of focus takes place between verses 12 and 13. The writer moves from the written Word of God to the Living Word. The purpose of the written Word is to bring us face-to-face with the Living Word:

> Nothing in all creation is hidden from God. *Everything is naked and exposed* before *his eyes*, and *he is the one* to whom we are accountable. (Hebrews 4:13 NLT, emphasis added)

The purpose of the written Word is to put the spotlight solely on the Lord and to reveal to us that there is nothing He does not see. There is an appointed day and time when everyone will give an account to the Living Word.

Knowingly or unknowingly, this is precisely why many people have chosen not to spend any time in the written Word of God. When you sit down to read the Word, it won't be long before you discover that the Word is reading you. It is a very sobering moment when one gets a revelation that secret sin on earth is an open scandal in heaven. God audits everything we do. There is nothing hidden from His sight. You can take that to the bank.

To the person who has not received and accepted Jesus Christ as their Lord and Savior, this verse can create a lot of anxiety—and it should. It will not be a pleasant moment for them when the "appointed day" arrives. There will be judgment followed by eternal separation from God:

> Then Death and Hades were cast into the lake of fire. This is the second death. And anyone not found written in the Book of Life was cast into the lake of fire. (Revelation 20:14–15 NKJV).

This does not sound like a happy ending for the nonbeliever.

Don't forget that the purpose of the written Word is to turn our focus to Jesus. Through the written Word, we discover why the Word became flesh and dwelt among us. He came to forgive us of our sins and give us an abundant life (John 10:10 NKJV). The Word (Jesus) took our place on the cross, bore our sins, died our death, and then conquered death and the grave so we can live.

If you have accepted the Lord's invitation to life, the fruit of this verse will be peace because the written Word reveals the goodness and grace of the Living Word. When we become students of the written Word, we find there is more grace in God than there is sin in us. The written Word reveals the identity of Jesus, and when we discover His identity, we will know who we are:

> As He is, so are we in this world. (1 John 4:17 NKJV)

The Living Word Wields the Written Word

In Luke 4, we find the Living Word (Jesus) engaged in spiritual combat with the devil. Jesus could have annihilated him with just His presence, but His choice of weapon was the sword of the Spirit. This is the written Word of God. Because Jesus is our supreme example for everything, it would be wise to pay close attention to how He used the written Word to defend Himself from Satan's assault and as an offensive weapon to repel Satan.

The public ministry of Jesus began with His baptism (Luke 3:21–22 NKJV). When He came up out of the water, heaven opened, and God spoke these words:

> You are My beloved Son; in You I am well pleased.
> (Luke 3:22 NKJV)

This was an audible voice. Everyone heard it, including the devil.

Immediately following His baptism, Jesus (the Living Word) was led by the Spirit into the wilderness where He was tempted by the devil for forty days. Jesus had eaten nothing during this entire period of time. This is the opportunity the devil had been looking for. He tried to seduce Jesus by taking advantage of his physical weakness and hunger:

> The Devil, *playing on his hunger*, gave the first test: "*Since* you're God's Son, command this stone to turn into a loaf of bread." (Luke 4:3 MSG, emphasis added)

This is one of the best, if not the best, renderings of this verse. The devil tried to get Jesus to use His identity to satisfy His needs. "You have not eaten anything for forty days. You are hungry. You are the Son of God. You are the Living Word. Go for it." This is the same tactic he used on Adam and Eve in the Garden of Eden. Satan planted the thought in their minds that maybe God did not say what they thought He said, "Has God indeed said?" (Genesis 3:1 NKJV). These words sounded so benign and nonthreatening, but they could not see the hooks Satan had camouflaged in his bait. Here is something we need to always keep on the front burners of our minds: words are seeds (Luke 8:11 NKJV). The seed that the devil planted would ultimately produce a crop failure for Adam—and for the entire world.

It is so important that we pay close attention to how Jesus responds to the shenanigans Satan is trying to pull on Him. He draws the sword of the Spirit, which is the Word of God. Without any hesitation, Jesus (the Living Word) quotes Deuteronomy 8:3; the written Word: "It is written, 'Man shall not live by bread alone, but by every word of God'" (NKJV). The devil had no response and no defense against the Word of God. Jesus used the very weapon that He has given to us so we can successfully defend ourselves against the devil's attacks.

The devil does not wave the white flag easily. After showing Jesus all the kingdoms of the world, the devil promised to give them to Him—with one condition. Jesus must bow down and worship him. Once again, Jesus did not hesitate:

> Get behind Me, Satan! For it is written, "You shall worship the Lord your God, and Him only you shall serve." (Luke 4:8 NKJV)

The Living Word quotes the written Word again (Deuteronomy 6:13). Are you beginning to see how important it is for us to put on the whole armor of God and to take the sword of the Spirit, which is the Word of God? Jesus is modeling for us how to fight and win in spiritual warfare by using the armor and weaponry God has made available for His children.

Satan takes Jesus to Jerusalem and sets Him on the pinnacle of the temple. He says to Jesus, "Since You are the Son of God, jump off." What he says next is mind-boggling. The devil has been taking a licking by the sword of the Spirit, but he has an idea. He would use the sword of the Spirit on the Living Word. He quotes Psalm 91:11–12 (NKJV), but he cunningly omits these words: "To keep you in all your ways." He purposefully misquoted the written Word. The devil knows how powerful the written Word of God is. He has been wounded by it innumerable times. As a matter of fact, he has already been totally defeated:

> Therefore submit to God. Resist the devil and he
> will flee from you. (James 4:7 NKJV)

Taking our stand on the Word of God is how we submit to God. When we do, Satan has no recourse but to flee.

How did Jesus respond to the devil's misuse of the sword of the Word? He parried his thrust and countered with the two-edged sword of truth. Jesus quotes Deuteronomy 6:16:

> It has been said, "You shall not tempt the Lord your
> God." (Luke 4:12 NKJV)

> Now when the devil had ended every temptation,
> he departed from Him until an opportune time.
> (Luke 4:13 NKJV)

We must never let down our guards. Just because we win a battle, it does not mean the war is over. The devil may flee, but he will always be looking for just the right opportunity to ambush us again:

> Stay alert! Watch out for your great enemy, the
> devil. He prowls around like a roaring lion, looking
> for someone to devour. (1 Peter 5:8 NLT)

Be vigilant. Stay on your spiritual toes! It is dangerous to become complacent, especially after being victorious over the enemy in a particular area of your life. The devil is always lurking in the shadows, disguised as a roaring lion. He will be constantly looking for another opportune time to bushwhack you.

When the devil saw that he was no match for the Living Word, he left until the next opportunity presented itself. Jesus chose the written Word as His weapon of choice—the sword of the Spirit. The devil is an illegitimate king of the beast, but Jesus is the legitimate King of kings. He has never lost a battle, and He never will. Here is some even better news: Jesus has already won the war! It is finished.

The Written Word is God's Breath

The written Word is not simply a book that tells us about God; it actually contains God. His breath is embedded in his Word:

> God has transmitted his very substance into every Scripture, for it is God-breathed. It will empower you by its instruction and correction, giving you the strength to take the right direction and lead you deeper into the path of godliness. Then you will be God's servant, fully mature and perfectly prepared to fulfill any assignment God gives you. (2 Timothy 3:16–17 TPT)

The written Word is God's breath. Read it and know that you are eating the bread of life and smelling the very breath of God. You are being resuscitated by God's life. This is exactly what happened when God breathed His life into Adam—he became a living soul (Genesis 2:7 NKJV).

The Greek word for *inspiration* (*Theopneustos*) literally means "inspired by God." It comes from *Theos*, the name for God, and *pneo* meaning "to breathe." In Christian theology, this is called inspiration of the scriptures. This separates the written Word of God from all other written material. The same God who breathed life into Adam is the One who put life into the written Word, making it the sword of the Spirit. "He transmitted his very substance into every scripture." The written Word is God's breath. Having a sound and healthy theology concerning the inspiration of the scriptures is very important, but the reality of it in our lives is even better.

This is precisely why the Word of God is so devastating to the enemy of our souls. When we use the sword of the Spirit to defend ourselves from his attacks and as an offensive weapon to rout him and his demonic forces, we are assured victory. And even more importantly, God gets the glory.

This is the purpose and power of the Word we talked about earlier in this chapter. When we wield the sword of the Spirit during spiritual conflicts, we are actually putting the breath of God in the face of the devil. He knows the smell of God's breath. Satan has already gotten a taste of what it is like to go toe-to-toe with God. He came out on the short end of the stick. The devil knows he cannot win when his adversary fights with the sword of the Spirit. He is praying (pun intended) that we never know.

The Written Word is Eternal

> The grass withers and the flowers fade, but the word
> of our God stands forever. (Isaiah 40:8 NLT)

I wonder what Isaiah meant when he said the Word of our God will stand forever. Do you suppose that he was saying the Word of God was eternal? I think the answer to that question is obviously yes. Since the written Word is the very essence of God—and God is eternal—it is impossible for His Word to have a beginning or an end. Because that is true, we have every right to expect God's Word to accomplish today what it has accomplished throughout time:

> For I am the Lord, I do not change. (Malachi 3:6 NKJV)

If God cannot change neither can His Word:

> Your eternal word, O Lord, stands firm in heaven. (Psalm 119:89 NLT)

The written Word will stand forever because it is the very breath of God.

There are only two things in this world we can tag as being eternal: people and the Word of God. Everything else will be consumed by fire at an appointed time. Jesus said this about His Word never ending:

> Heaven and earth will disappear, but *my words will never disappear.* (Matthew 24:35 NLT, emphasis added)

Since God transmitted His very substance into His Word, it will be around for as long as God exists. That should put a smile on your face and hope in your heart.

The majority of humanity is wearing themselves to a frazzle by trying to build lives without the support of a firm foundation. This is why we see so many people crumbling and imploding every day. Drug abuse and the suicide rates are escalating to incredible proportions. People have given up on living and opted for existing.

Nothing—and I mean absolutely nothing—can provide the proper foundation for building one's life on than the Word and His Word. No one in their right mind would argue against the importance of having an adequate foundation laid before building a structure, but not thinks about firm footing when it comes to building our personal lives. Jesus had this to say about the importance of having the right foundation:

> Anyone who listens to my teaching (word) and follows it is wise, like a person who builds a house (life) on solid rock. Though the rain comes in torrents and the floodwaters rise and the winds beat against that house (life), it won't collapse because it is built on bedrock (the Word of God). But anyone who hears my teaching (word) and doesn't obey it is foolish, like a person who builds a house (life) on sand. *When* the rains and floods come and the winds beat against that house (life), it will collapse with a mighty crash. (Matthew 7:24–27 NLT, emphasis added)

Jesus is not talking about a physical structure. He is talking about a person's life. He did not say *if* the rains and winds come. He said *when* they come. There will be many storms that will buffet our lives as we make our way from the cradle to the grave. If we have chosen to build our lives on a foundation other than Christ and His Word, failure and destruction are givens.

The Word of God provide us with a firm foundation, and it gives us purpose and meaning. What we need to do is find the right answer to this question: What is the purpose of life? If we get it right, everything begins to open up. If the Word of God is eternal—and we know it is because God transmitted His very essence into it—then our answer needs to come from the Word. The purpose of life is revealed in Jesus's prayer in John 17:

> And this is eternal life, that *they may know You*, the only true God, and Jesus Christ whom You have sent. (John 17:3 NKJV, emphasis added)

Here it is in flashing lights. Everything flows out of knowing our identities in Christ. It does not come from knowing about Him. The meaning of life comes from knowing Him. Until that is settled, an individual will never find true purpose and meaning in their lives.

It Is Time We Feast on Daily Bread

God has given His written Word to be our daily bread and not some fancy dessert to be served on special occasions. If we have been faithfully eating His Word on a daily basis, the people we come in contact with will be able to smell it on our breath. The smell of the Word of God on our lips cannot be hidden from our friends or foes.

CHAPTER 11

BATTLE READY

There is much more we would like to say about this, but it is difficult to explain, especially since you are spiritually dull and don't seem to listen. *You have been believers so long now that you ought to be teaching others.* Instead, you need someone to teach you again the basic things about God's Word. *You are like babies who need milk and cannot eat solid food.* For someone who lives on milk is still an infant and doesn't know how to do what is right. Solid food is for those who are mature, *who through training* have the skill to recognize the difference between right and wrong.
—Hebrews 5:11–14 (NLT, emphasis added)

You can hear and feel the writer's fingernails scraping the chalkboard when you read these four verses. They make you a little fidgety. The community of faith is chock-full of believers who are still nursing on a bottle and wearing spiritual diapers when they should be feasting on solid food—and it is all because of a lack of practice.

Being equipped for battle and being ready for battle may not be the same thing. Even if we are equipped with the best and most effective weaponry of warfare, if we don't know how to use these weapons efficiently, the chances are good we will become casualties. Being battle ready requires training and a lot of practice in real-life situations.

Back in the late sixties, I enlisted in the army for a three-year stint. As a young nineteen-year-old, I had no clue what I had signed up for. It did not take long for me to smell the coffee. This was no game we were playing. The Vietnam War was escalating rapidly, and we were being prepared for jungle warfare. My military occupational specialty (MOS) was 11B1P—airborne infantry.

During basic training, we spent a lot of time getting in top physical condition. We were taught how to use the M-14 rifle and properly throw a hand grenade. We were exposed to many types of weapons. Once basic training was over, we were transferred to AIT (advance infantry training), and our preparation for jungle warfare became more intense. We exchanged our M-14 rifles for M-16s. Countless hours were spent learning how to break it down, clean it, and reassemble it in short order.

A lot of our training took place in the wet, mossy areas of Louisiana. This was intentionally designed to get us prepared as much as possible for the jungles of Vietnam. We were exposed to different types of booby traps that we would encounter and the tactics of the enemy we would be facing. During live-fire training, we would crawl on our bellies as live rounds were fired over our heads and explosives were being detonated in encased shields close by. Even though we knew the chances of someone being hit by a live round was next to nil, no one had to tell us to keep our heads down—even though our drill instructors kept yelling at us to stay as low as possible.

Once we completed AIT, those with 1P in their MOS were flown to Georgia for jump school. The training was both physical and mental. We jumped off of short concrete walls to practice our PLFs (parachute landing falls) before we were moved to thirty-four-foot towers. Equipped with a parachute harness strapped to a static line, we jumped to get a small taste of what it would feel like when our parachutes deployed when we jumped from an airplane. To enhance the experience, we were hoisted to the top of a two-hundred-fifty-foot tower and then dropped. This gave us some exposure to what it would be like jumping from a height, and it introduced us to what it would feel like when we landed. We did not just talk about weapons; we practiced using them. We did not just talk about jumping out of planes; we actually jumped.

When we graduated from jump school, we were flown to Vietnam. Once there, we received a week of in-country training. We saw firsthand what the jungles of Vietnam were like. We felt the heat, the leeches, and the rain. We handled the booby traps we would encounter. We learned as much as we possibly could about what the indigenous people were like. Once this seven-day period was over, we were flown by helicopters to our units in the field. Equipped and trained with the best weaponry, we were ready to engage the enemy. We were ready for combat, and that did not take long. Why were we exposed to such intense training? This rigorous preparation was to give us a better chance for survival. We would be facing life-and-death situations. Our lives depended on it—and so did the lives of our fellow comrades. To not prepare would have been suicidal. War is not a game.

Spiritual warfare is not a game either. Far too many believers are being slaughtered on the spiritual battlefield because they have not received proper training—if any at all. Even though the children of God are in possession of superior weaponry, the majority are not being trained for war. They are equipped, but they are not prepared to face the enemy. That is a recipe for disaster.

This is exactly what the writer of Hebrews was talking about:

> Even though you have been believers for a long time, and should be equipping others for warfare, you need to be taught the basics of the Word of God (the sword of God) again; and again, and again. (Hebrews 5:12 NKJV)

Becoming Battle Ready

Spiritual warfare has intensified, and it is going to continue to escalate. Bringing our new creation thinking into alignment with our new creation identities will determine if we win or lose in the spiritual conflicts that we find ourselves in on a regular basis. The devil is focused on taking us out. If he can't eliminate us, he will do everything he can to bring us to the point of surrender. The more we prepare for these engagements, the more effective and victorious we will be.

This is why the Word of God instructs us to put on the full armor of God. We need to be fully dressed for battle. The enemy is always looking for those unprotected, exposed areas in our lives that he can take advantage of. Being arrayed in the full armor of God makes us impregnable and unconquerable. No weapon formed against us will succeed (Isaiah 54:17 NLT). That is incredible news. The devil has nothing in his arsenal that can compete with the full armor of God.

Truth is the devil's greatest threat. Jesus said this about our enemy:

> You are of your farther the devil, and the desires of your father you want to do. He was a murderer from the beginning, and *does not stand in the truth*, because there is *no truth in him*. When he speaks a lie, he speaks from his own resources, for *he is a liar and the father of it*. (John 8:44 NKJV, emphasis added)

The devil may be the master of deception and the father of lies, but he is no match for the truth. We are girded with the belt of truth (Ephesians 6:14, JKJV). Since our enemy has no defense against the truth, it would be advantageous for us to know what truth is. The Word of God tells us:

> I am the way, *the truth*, and the life. (John 14:6
> NKJV, emphasis added)

These are the words of Jesus himself. Hang onto that nugget as we connect it to what Jesus prayed in John 17:

> Make them holy by *your truth*; teach them *your*
> *word, which is truth.* (John 17:17 NLT, emphasis
> added)

Jesus says unequivocally that He is the truth, and in His prayer, He says that the Word of God is truth. To get the full picture, let's connect one more dot. John begins his Gospel with these words:

> In the beginning *the Word* already existed. *The*
> *Word* was with God, and *the Word* was God. (John
> 1:1 NLT, emphasis added)

> So *the Word* became human and made his home
> among us. He was full of unfailing love and
> faithfulness. And we saw his glory, the glory of
> the Father's one and only son. (John 1:14 NLT,
> emphasis added)

As a new creation in Christ, we are completely enshrouded in Him. Christ is our belt of truth! When this becomes a reality, we are ready for battle.

Being in Christ places us in right standing with God. We don't stand in our own righteousness, which leaves us exposed and vulnerable when we are assaulted by the enemy of our souls. Righteousness is the breastplate that prevents our feelings, thoughts, and actions from going off the rails during spiritual conflicts. This knowledge keeps us together when we feel we are coming apart. If you have accepted Jesus Christ as your Lord and Savior, the breastplate of right standing with God belongs to you. Put it on with confidence:

> For God was in Christ, reconciling (exchanging) the world to himself, no longer counting people's sins against them. For God made Christ, who never sinned, to be the offering for our sin, *so that we could be made right* (righteous, right standing) *with God through Christ.* (2 Corinthians 5:19; 21 NLT, emphasis added)

As new creations, we are righteous. This is not because of anything we do for the Lord; it is because of what He has done for us. When putting on the breastplate of righteousness becomes more important than just having a discussion in hermeneutics (biblical interpretation) about what it means to being a living reality in us, we are ready for battle.

If there is any single thing that is conspicuous by its absence in the lives of believers today, it is peace. Anywhere we choose to stand is shaky ground if we are not standing in peace. Peace is what gives us stability. That is why Paul tells us to make sure we are wearing battle-tested footwear. The chances of us running from battle increase if we are unstable. The only possible way to stand without wavering when we are fighting for our lives is to have our feet properly shod with the preparation of the Gospel of peace (Ephesians 6:15 NKJV).

Peace and fear cannot coexist:

> For God has not given us *a spirit* of fear and timidity, but of power, love, and self-discipline. (2 Timothy 1:7 NLT, emphasis added)

Pay close attention to what Paul said about fear and timidity to young Timothy. Fear is a spirit, and it is not from God. If the source of a spirit of fear is not from God, there is only one other source.

And your answer is? The purpose of a spirit of fear is to rob us of our peace:

> The thief does not come except *to steal* and *to kill*, and *to destroy*. (John 10:10 NKJV)

This is Satan's job description. He has had a lot of success in stealing our peace because we do not know who our peace is:

> For He Himself (Jesus) is our peace. (Ephesians 2:14 NKJV, emphasis added)

Here is a news flash: Christ is our life. He is our everything:

> When *Christ who is our life* appears, then you also will appear with Him in glory. (Colossians 3:4 NKJV, emphasis added)

> For *in him* we live and move and have our being. (Acts 17:28 NKJV, emphasis added)

This is why it is imperative for believers to know who they are and what they have in Christ. To not know that can be devastating. We need to start thinking like the new creations we are.

The next time you find yourself under assault in your thought life, focus on this scripture:

> And *the peace of God*, which surpasses all understanding, will guard *your hearts* and *minds* through Christ Jesus. (Philippians 4:7 NKJV, emphasis added)

This verse tells us there are two things that God's peace protects. The first thing God's peace guards is our hearts, which includes our feelings and emotions. It is easy for our emotions to override the truth if we panic. Feelings may be real, but they may not be true. I can feel that God does not love me. My feelings are real, but they are certainly not true. God's love for His children is unwavering.

The second thing this verse tells us is that the peace of God guards our minds, which includes our thoughts and the way we think. Our thoughts and feelings will be challenged the most during spiritual conflicts. The enemy knows that if he can infiltrate them, he can do some damage. However, when we know that we are at peace with God, we can find comfort and protection in the peace of God:

> Therefore, having been *justified by faith, we have peace with God* through our Lord Jesus Christ. (Romans 5:1 NKJV, emphasis added)

When this becomes a living reality, we are prepared for battle.

Satan has gained a lot of territory on the battlefield (between our ears) because he has been able to convince a lot of Christians that they have been shortchanged when it comes to faith. We think, *If I only had more faith* or *If I had the faith that person has.* Many people think they do not have enough of what they need: faith. All this negative self-talk produces is more defeat. Let me give you some phenomenal news. The faith we have is not even ours. The faith we are in possession of is His faith. We live by His faith. You did not misread that. We live by the faith of another:

> I have been crucified with Christ; it is no longer I who live but Christ lives in me; and the life which I now live in the flesh *I live by faith in the Son of God* who loved me and gave Himself for me. (Galatians 2:20 NKJV, emphasis added)

This verse seems to confirm what many Christians believe: we need more faith. The King James translates Galatians 2:20 this way: "I live *by the faith of the Son of God.*" This is probably the most accurate translation. Living by the faith of the Son of God instead of by my faith in the Son of God coordinates with scriptures that speak of our oneness with our Creator. Apart from Him, we have nothing, including life. If God were to take everything from us that did not belong to us, what would we have left? Even the breath in our lungs does not belong to us.

Since we have become partakers of His divine nature (2 Peter 1:4), His faith is our faith shield. This is why it has the ability to quench all the flaming arrows the enemy shoots at us. Our shield of faith protects us, and it protects the other pieces of armor as well. It is fascinating that the shield of faith is the only piece of armor used primarily for defensive purposes. In the heat of battle, the Roman soldiers would interlock their shields to form a wall of defense. This maneuver protected them from flaming arrows and provided protection for their fellow comrades. This is desperately needed in the community of faith. A wall of faith makes the whole body of believers safer and stronger. Once we take up our shields of faith, we are ready to take the fight to the enemy.

The importance of proper headgear in contact sports cannot be overemphasized. Can you imagine the damage that would occur if players in the NFL did not wear helmets? Football players still receive head injuries—even though their heads are protected by the best head protection money can buy. I don't think anyone would argue that helmets are not essential for contact sports. I have a few adjectives I could use for the person who thinks helmets are not necessary, but I will keep them to myself.

Having on the proper headgear for spiritual battle is incredibly important. This is why Paul tells us to put on the helmet of salvation (Ephesians 6:17 NKJV). When we find ourselves in the heat of a spiritual battle, our thoughts must be protected at all costs. We will win or lose the fight in our thought lives. The devil will do everything in his power to plant unhealthy thoughts in our heads with his lies. Many believers are AWOL (absent without leave) today because they did not have on the full armor of God when they were ambushed by the devil. When we have on the helmet of salvation, we are able to do what Paul told the church in Corinth to do: capture every thought and bring them into captivity (2 Corinthians 10:5 NKJV). The next time you find yourself in spiritual conflict, remind yourself of what truth is: "But we have the mind of Christ" (1 Corinthians 2:16 NKJV). We are battle ready when we are wearing the helmet of salvation.

Reasons for Not Being Battle Ready

Normal Christians are suspicious about supernatural experiences because they don't have them. Their experiences, or the lack thereof, set the standard for what they believe. They have no awareness that their lives are in jeopardy because they do not know about spiritual warfare or the armor of God.

A child of God who is not ready for battle may have never been taught that they are in a battle. I find it amazing that a large percentage of believers do not know they could and should practice their faith. I encounter Christians all the time who tell me they have never heard of spiritual warfare. To them, it is something that happens in a dimension that is unfathomable. They are totally oblivious to the fact that the struggle they are in is taking place in a six-inch space between their ears. Is there any wonder why there are so many casualties in the family of faith?

Some Christians may not be ready for battle because of ignorance. They just don't know. Being ignorant about something is not a sin or a crime. However, remaining ignorant is a different story. Ignorance can be remedied by information. The motivation for writing this book is *new creation thinking*. It is time for the body of Christ to wake up, put on the full armor of God, and fight the good fight of faith. We are living in a day and time when spiritual ignorance is not bliss. It could cost you everything.

Not being ready for war could be because of disobedience, a lack of self-governance, or simply laziness. Whatever the reason, the outcome can be devastating.

New Creation Thinking

One of Satan's primary weapons is deceit. His goal is to get believers to accept something that is false or invalid as being true and valid. He has had a lot of experience concealing and misrepresenting the truth. Satan wants to convince us that the bad and unhealthy thoughts that slowly work their ways through our heads belong to us. He knows guilt will quickly follow if we own them as ours.

If we are serious about living victorious Christian lives, we will start working harder to overcome our thought issues, which will eventually wear us out (Daniel 7:25 NKJV). The devil will start with small things so we will become conditioned and more susceptible to his bigger lies. Oftentimes, he will start with thoughts that we do not recognize as being destructive, which he did with Eve: "Has God really said?" (Genesis 3:1 NKJV). We certainly know how that turned out, don't we?

When we begin to think like the new creations we are, the devil is no match for us—and he knows it. That does not mean we will go through all of our battles unscathed. As long as we are in this world, we will encounter momentary defeats, setbacks, cuts, scrapes, and bruises. It goes with the territory. This only makes us stronger in our faith.

Children of God who are settled and confident in their new creation identities will refuse to give up or give in when they are fully engaged in battle. The words *quit* and *surrender* are not in their vocabularies:

> He (Jesus) died for everyone so that those who *receive his new life* will no longer live for themselves.

Instead, they will live for Christ, who died and was raised for them. So we have stopped evaluating others from a human point of view. At one time we thought of Christ merely from a human point of view. How differently we know him now! This means that anyone who belongs to Christ has become *a new person. The old life is gone; a new life has begun.* (2 Corinthians 5:15–17 NLT, emphasis added)

Focus on the last nine words in 1 John 4:17 and look at them in the light of the three verses we just quoted from 2 Corinthians: "As He is, so are we in this world." This verse does not say, "As He was." Because we are in Him, we are not who we were either. Our old lives are gone, and our new lives have begun.

Whoever we were before we accepted and received Jesus as our Lord and Savior no longer exists—and the old people we were will never return! It is time for the body of Christ to start thinking like the new creations we have become. It may feel awkward at first, but growth usually does. This may be the right time to give you a warning. When you become convinced about your new identity, don't be surprised if you hear some Christians saying that you are conceited:

But thank God! He has made us his captives and continues to lead us along in Christ's triumphal procession. Now he uses us to spread the knowledge of Christ everywhere, like a sweet perfume. Our lives are a Christ-like fragrance rising up to God. But this fragrance is perceived differently by those who are being saved and by those who are perishing. To those who are perishing, we are a dreadful smell of death and doom. But to those who are being saved, we are a life-giving perfume. (2 Corinthians 2:14–16 NLT)

When we begin to think like the new creations we have become in Christ, people will be able to smell God's life in us—both the unsaved and saved.

CHAPTER 12

LET THIS MIND BE IN YOU

—

And consider the example that Jesus, the Anointed One, has
set before us. *Let his mindset become your motivation.*
—Philippians 2:5 (TPT, emphasis added)

f I had the assignment of picking a verse that defines what it
means to be a follower of Jesus Christ, it would be this one. In the
New King James Version, it is rendered this way: "Let this mind
be in you which was also in Christ Jesus" (Philippians 2:5 NKJV).

Our motivation for living godly lives while we are on this side
of eternity is to make God known to a world that desperately needs
Him. To do this, we must appropriate the mindset of Jesus. The only
way this is possible is when we purposely set our minds on what He
sets His mind on. In other words, we must think the way He thinks.
He is our example, and we need to pay close attention to how He
thought because it determined how He lived.

Is this really possible? This is out of the realm of normal
Christian thinking. Believing that we can think like Jesus has a
slight ring of heresy to it. Who do we think we are? That could very
well be our problem. We do not know who we are. We still think
like who we were and not like who we have become in Christ. I am

convinced this is the primary reason. We certainly could not think like Jesus before we were saved because we were spiritually dead, which means we were unplugged from the power source of life. When we accepted and received Jesus as our Lord and Savior, we were spiritually plugged into His very nature, giving us the ability to do what we could not do without Him, which is to think like He does (2 Peter 1:4 NKJV). As a matter of fact, as a new creation, we do have the mind of Christ:

> For who has known the mind of the Lord that he may instruct Him? *But we have the mind of Christ.* (1 Corinthians 2:16 NKJV, emphasis added)

Allow me to put my own spin on an iconic slogan that has been around for over four decades: Whatever you do, don't let a good mind go to waste. As a new creation in Christ, you now have a choice that you did not have before. You can think the same way you did before you became a child of God—or you can appropriate what you have been given as a child of God: the mind of Christ.

New Creation Thinking Must Be Intentional

New creation thinking is something that must be done intentionally. It will not happen naturally or be an easy assignment. This is why we are to pay close attention to the example Jesus set for us. Having the mindset of Jesus simply means setting our minds on the very things He focused on. It is an act of our wills. Jesus made it possible for us to become new creations. It is time to bring our new creation thinking into alignment with our new creation identities. Always keep this in mind: God would never tell us to do something if it were not possible for us to do. "As He is, so are we in this world" (1 John 4:17 NKJV). If this is true—and it is—then it is possible for us to think the way He does.

New creation thinking must be intentional on our part because we are constantly being bombarded with distractions. A distraction does not have to be something that is bad in and of itself. It can be anything that prevents us from setting our minds (mindset) on living life the way Jesus did. If the enemy is able to get us to shift our focus from Christ—and get us to set our sights on a world that is temporal—he will be successful in distracting us from what is eternal. An inordinate affection for the world will get us preoccupied with temporal things. If this ever happens, our earthly lives will become more important to us than our heavenly lives:

> Casting all your care (distractions) upon Him, for He cares for you. (1 Peter 5:7 NKJV, emphasis added)

God gives us permission to saddle Him with our distractions.

We must never underestimate how the way we think influences the way we live. Whatever you set your mind on will determine the way you live—always! How was Jesus able to live the way He did? Because He kept His focus on His Father:

> So Jesus explained, "I tell you the truth, the Son can do nothing by himself. *He does only what he sees the Father doing.* Whatever the Father does, the Son also does." (John 5:19 NKJV, emphasis added)

How was Jesus able to do what His Father did? He kept His mind set on His Father. And what did Paul tell us in Philippians?

> *Consider the example Jesus*, the Anointed One, has set before us. *Let His mindset become your motivation.* (Philippians 2:5 TPT, emphasis added)

Thinking like Jesus must be intentional. It is a matter of focus.

New Creation Thinking Will Determine How We Live

I was a mischievous knucklehead while I was growing up. It was not uncommon for a teacher or other adult to say, "What were you thinking, young man?" This question was usually asked after I had done something that I thought was creative. I was a *very* creative young knucklehead. The thing that kept getting me in to trouble was what I chose to set my mind on. I had an unhealthy mindset. My focus was not where it should have been, and that kept me in hot water.

A mind set on the flesh will lead to a life that is ungodly. A mind set on the things of the Spirit will lead to a godly life. Having the right mindset is always our choice. We decide what we focus on. The way we think will determine how we live our lives. Paul addresses this issue in the letter he wrote to the believers in Rome:

> For those who live according to the flesh *set their minds on the things of the flesh*, but those who live according to the Spirit, the things of the *Spirit*. (Romans 8:5 NKJV, emphasis added)

We are not left to figure out on our own how to live lives that are in keeping with our new creation identities. The Word of God makes it very clear. People who choose to set their minds on the flesh (carnal things, temporal things) will live accordingly. Those who have chosen to set their minds on the things of the Spirit will live like the new creations they have become in Christ. The Word of God makes it blatantly clear that we will live according to what we set our minds on.

Paul continues writing about the importance of setting our minds on what is good and healthy:

> For to be carnally (fleshly) minded is death, but to be spiritually minded is life and peace. Because

the carnal mind is enmity against God; for it is not subject to the law of God, or indeed can be. So then, those who are in the flesh cannot please God. *But you are not in the flesh but in the Spirit*, if indeed the Spirit of God dwells in you. Now if anyone does not have the Spirit of Christ, he is not His. (Romans 8:6–9 NKJV, emphasis added)

Have you had a born-from-above experience with Christ? If you have, the Word of God (truth) clearly states that you are no longer in the flesh, and it is impossible for you to return to the flesh. It is possible to set your mind on the flesh, and if this is the choice you make, you will be living by the flesh. Living *by the flesh* and being *in the flesh* are not the same thing. Before you were saved, you were in the flesh, and there was nothing you could do to get out of it. But after you were born-again, you were taken out of the flesh and placed into the Spirit. This is a miracle. It is impossible to leave the Spirit and reenter the flesh. If it were possible, we would be able to annul a miracle. Being born from above is a miracle. We also need to understand that if setting our minds on the flesh is the choice we make, we will suffer the consequences of those decisions—just like the individual who is not saved. Even though the scriptures declare it in living color, this is outside the parameters of normal Christian thinking.

Physical Birth Determines Our Old Creation Identities

How did you become a human being? I realize that question may sound strange to most people because the answer is obvious: we were born human beings. It was our physical birth that made that determination. When we came into this world, no one had to pray that we would grow up to be human beings. That was a given, and it required no prayer. It did take prayer and a lot of discipline for most of us to mature in our identities as humans.

There have been times when many of us have acted in ways that brought into question what species we belonged to—some of us more than others. I am thinking of my brother, Keith. The point that I am trying to establish is that our physical birth is what made us humans—period. No matter how hard we try, we will never become more human. Nothing we can do will ever make us more than what we were born as. Even when we act in ways that are not becoming of human beings, it does not negate our identities as humans. We are simply acting in ways that are not in keeping with who we are.

The maturation process for a person is in stages: baby, child, boy or girl, youth, man or woman. During this process of developing, the baby never becomes more human. They simply become a mature manifestation of what they were born as.

From conception to birth is a miracle. Life is a miracle. This may sound elementary to many Christians—as well as being a little ridiculous—but it gives us something to wrap our minds around when we think about our spiritual births.

Spiritual Birth Determines Our New Creation Identities

How did we become children of God? We became brand-new creations the same way we became humans when we were physically born. We had a second birthday. This is exactly what Jesus told a man by the name of Nicodemus:

> Most assuredly I say to you, *unless one is born again*, he cannot see the kingdom of God. (John 3:3 NKJV, emphasis added)

Because Nicodemus only had the natural mindset that he was born with, he could not comprehend anything in the spiritual realm. He was unable to see the kingdom that Jesus was talking about—the kingdom of God. This is obvious by his response:

> How can a man be born when he is old? *Can he enter a second time into his mother's womb and be born?* (John 3:4 NKJV, emphasis added)

Jesus was talking about being born spiritually. Nicodemus was thinking about being born naturally. He did not have the ability to set his mind on the things of the spirit. He did not have the foggiest idea how someone could be born from above. Old creation thinking is limited to the earthly realm. It requires a new mind to comprehend the things of the Spirit. If you have had a born-from-above experience with Jesus Christ, then you have that ability. It is time to set our minds and affections on things above—even though we are living in this world below (Colossians 3:2 NKJV).

There is nothing we can do that will make us more of a child of God than we were when we were born again. This flies in the face of normal Christianity. We have been convinced that if we work really hard, do enough good things, and faithfully follow a rigid set of ecclesiastical laws, we will become more than we are. Those things may help us mature in our faith lives, but they will have no effect on our identities whatsoever. We will never become more of a child of God by our works or anything else. Our new creation identities were determined the moment we had our second birthday. Maturing as children of God comes from practicing the fundamentals of faith, but it contributes nothing to us being children of God (Hebrews 5:12–14 NKJV). We are as holy now as we will be when we get to heaven. We are as righteous as we will ever be. This truth flies in the face of our experiences and sounds heretical to most Christians.

In Matthew's account of the birth narrative of our Savior, he gives us some insight into this incredible truth about birth manifesting our identities:

> Where is He *who has been born King* of the Jews? For we have seen His star in the East and have come to worship Him (Matthew 2:2 NKJV, emphasis added)

Jesus was not born a prince and then became king when he grew up. His physical birth manifested His spiritual identity. Jesus was King in the heavenly realm long before He expressed Himself as King in the earthly realm. You may be thinking, *Yes, but the birth of Jesus was a miracle.* You are right—and so was your spiritual birth.

In His humanity, Jesus grew and matured in His identity as King of kings and Lord of lords:

> Then He (Jesus) went down with them (Mary and Joseph) and came to Nazareth, and was subject to them, but His mother kept all these things in her heart. *And Jesus increased in wisdom and stature, and in favor with God and men.* (Luke 2:51–51 NKJV, emphasis added)

Even though Jesus knew who He was when He was twelve years old, the world was not ready for a twelve-year-old Messiah.

Resetting Our Mindsets

The first sentence in the introduction to this book was carefully thought out. It takes faith and a lot of courage to walk away from being an average Christian. Hopefully, by now, you see how true that is. There should be an obvious distinction between the lifestyle of a believer and that of an unbeliever. However, it is often difficult to tell the difference, and it is all because of mindset. New creation thinking will (and should) separate us from those who do not know Christ, and it should set us apart from normal Christians. It is possible for us to think like the new creations we have become in Jesus Christ, but it will take faith, a lot of courage, and some thick skin (2 Corinthians 5:17 NKJV). When you become convinced about your identity as a child of God, you may be considered conceited by those who have settled for being average Christians.

Children are told all the time that they can accomplish anything they set their minds to, but it takes determination and purposeful intent. A lot can be accomplished when there is singleness of vision and resolve. What is true in the natural is even more true in the spiritual. Since we have been born from above, we now have the ability to do what we were not able to do before. We can set our minds and affections on things above, but it takes a deliberate act of our wills. A spiritually minded person will discover what all of humanity is in search of: life and peace. It may be time for a "mind reset."

Resetting your mindset has the power to change you even if your circumstances do not. It can be the difference between living a victorious life or a defeated life. The way we think will affect the way we live. We are all living our lives today according to what we choose to focus on. The Word of God tells us that there are only two things that we can set our minds on: things of the flesh or things of the spirit (Romans 8:5–9 NKJV). If our mindsets are consumed by the flesh, the result will be death. If we intentionally set our minds on the things of the Spirit, we will experience life and peace (Romans 8:6 NKJV). The ball is in our court. I am convinced that most believers are not even aware they have a choice.

It is time to think about what we are thinking about. This is where we must begin if there is going to be a reset in our mindset. If what consumes our thoughts does not produce the fruit of life and peace, we need a reset. The next time you become aware that the thoughts flowing between your ears are not producing what God has promised to His children, immediately stop and declare, "These are not my thoughts. I refuse to own them." Immediately shift your focus toward God and His goodness—and then watch how faith replaces fear. It will help immensely if you sing a praise chorus, start quoting scriptures, or simply envision yourself sitting at the feet of Jesus. A picture is worth a thousand words. This is something that must be intentional and done out of your free will. It may take some time, but the more you practice your faith and resetting your mindset, the easier and quicker it will happen.

Don't Allow Your Experiences or Feelings to Trump Truth

> For God has not given us *a spirit of fear,* but of
> power and of love and of a sound mind. (2 Timothy
> 1:7 NKJV, emphasis added)

This verse is familiar to most people who attend a church service
with any regularity. They may not know the exact address of this
scripture, or quote it verbatim, but they can recite the spirit of it.
Sometimes it is helpful to pay attention to what a verse does not
say in order to see what it does say. Paul does not say that God has
not given us *the* spirit of fear; he calls it *a* spirit of fear. Why is this
important? *Fear is a spirit,* and it does not come from God. God is
not the source of a spirit of fear. If God is not the source, we are
left with only one other option. I am sure you can figure that out
without any help.

On numerous occasions, Jesus told His disciples, and others, not
to be afraid. Here is one of the many examples:

> But He (Jesus) said to them, "It is I; do not be
> afraid." (John 6:20 NKJV, emphasis added)

Here is something interesting that is worth paying attention to.
Jesus was always telling people not to be afraid, but He never told
anyone not to feel fear. Feeling fear and being full of fear are not the
same thing. Feeling fear can actually be a stimulus that activates our
resolve to overcome life-threatening situations. Feeling fear does not
mean we are faithless, but we do not want to succumb to a spirit of
fear and become fearful (full of fear).

What is true about fear is also true concerning temptation.
Being tempted and giving in to temptation are not the same thing.
Jesus was tempted just like we are, but He never took a bite of Satan's
bait. Temptation in and of itself is not sin; it is the bait the enemy
has chosen to use in his attempt to get us to bite. He knows our

vulnerability. There are consequences if we capitulate and succumb to his enticements.

What in the world do "feeling fear" and "being tempted" have to do with new creation thinking? I think that is a legitimate question for us to be asking. Let's place our feelings within the same context as we did with fear and temptation. Feeling that you do not measure up to what the Word of God says about you does not change or alter the truth of God in any way. You are who He says you are—no matter how you feel or what you think. The Word of God is what validates your new creation identity; it is not your feelings or what passes through your head. It is not uncommon to have feelings that challenge the truth.

God's Word says that we are holy—even though we may not feel holy. The Word of God says that we are righteous—even though we may not feel righteous. We now have a choice that we did not have before our born-from-above experience with Christ. We can embrace how God sees us or give in to our feelings and thoughts, which are constantly changing: "For I am the Lord, I do not change" (Malachi 3:6 NKJV). Since God can never change, truth can't either because His Word is the truth. Again, thinking like a child of God is not something that will happen automatically. It can happen, but it is a choice you will have to make.

Many Christians are not living up to their new creation identities because they are struggling with their thoughts. The conflict is coming from old creation thinking (who we used to be) instead of thinking like the new creations we have become in Christ. To complicate things even more, because our thoughts are real, we assume they are true. It is like feeling fear. Just because we feel fear, it does not mean our faith has failed us or that we are terrible Christians who will never be overcomers like other believers. These defeated brothers and sisters are allowing their experiences and feelings to override the truth about their new creation identities.

For the average Christian, their experiences and feelings outweigh the Word of God. Just because our thoughts and feelings are real does not make them true. Our feelings and thoughts must be judged by the truth, and the truth is the Word of God. Since the Word of God is truth, we are who He says we are—no matter how we struggle with our feelings and thoughts (John 17:17 NKJV).

It's okay to feel doubt at times, but we should not become doubtful (full of doubt). This does not mean something is wrong with you or that you are less valuable than other believers. If we allow this to happen, our lives will spiral out of control because we are being controlled by doubt. Don't allow anything or anyone to sit at the control panel of your life. That seat belongs to the Lord:

> And *consider the example that Jesus*, the Anointed One, has set before us. *Let his mindset become our motivation.* He existed in the form of God, yet he gave no thought to seizing equality with God as his supreme prize. Instead he emptied himself of his outward glory by reducing himself to the form of a lowly servant. *He became human.* He humbled himself and became vulnerable, choosing to be revealed as a man and was obedient. *He was a perfect example*, even in his death—a criminal's death by crucifixion. (Philippians 2:5–8 TPT, emphasis added)

> Let this mind be in you which was also in Christ Jesus. (Philippians 2:5 NKJV)

If we are going to experience the fullness of our birthright privileges as children of God, we must start thinking like the new creations we have become in Christ. This will not happen without a willful decision on our parts. Living with a heavenly mindset distinguishes us from being average Christians. When we set our minds on things above, we begin to live life from the inside out. That is new creation thinking.

EPILOGUE

For he (God) has rescued us from the kingdom of darkness
and transferred us into the Kingdom of his dear Son,
who purchased our freedom and forgave our sins.
—Colossians 1:13 (NLT, emphasis added)

The moment we accepted the Lord's invitation to life, we were moved from the kingdom of darkness and transferred into the kingdom of light. It is impossible for us to return to the darkness that we were delivered from because we have been made new creations. Our old selves could not share the life of Christ because it bore the corrupted seed of the first Adam. Corrupted seed cannot cohabit with incorruptible seed. This is why a person must be born from above before they can be in union with Christ.

As new creations in Christ, we bear the incorruptible seed of Jesus. He is called the last Adam. This makes us partakers of His divine nature (2 Peter 1:4 NKJV). Whether or not we live up to our calling as new creation beings, it will never change the truth of our new identities. However, it will rob us of the incredible lives that Jesus paid for with His life.

A Recipe for Failure

Many Christians never experience the "free indeed" life that Christ set us free to because of the way they think. It is a thinking problem. Believers know they are new creations in Christ because the Word of God says they are. That is not the issue. The conflict comes from not knowing that it is impossible to enjoy our new creation lives if we continue to think like who we were before Christ and not like who we are in Christ.

Most Christians are clueless because they have not been taught. How can you teach something you don't know? I had the honor of being taught by some incredible men of God, and I never heard much—or anything—about new creation thinking. Maybe they did mention it, but I did not have ears to hear. That is a real possibility. I certainly knew that I was saved and that I was going to heaven, but my experiences did not match up with a lot of scriptures that deal with our identities in Christ, especially this one:

> Therefore, if anyone is in Christ, he is a new creation (here comes the tough part of this verse), *old things have passed away, behold all things have become new.* (2 Corinthians 5:17 NKJV, emphasis added)

Even though I believed what that verse says, it was not my experience. If old things have passed away, then why do I still battle some of the same old things I struggled with before I became a Christian. At that time in my faith walk, I was totally unaware that I had to demand that my thinking must rise to the level of truth and not dumb down the truth to validate my experiences.

I was convinced that I was a new creation in Christ, but I tried to live my new life by old creation thinking. I was seeing 2 Corinthians 5:17 from a performance perspective and not from an identity perspective. My performance was not in sync with my identity as a child of God in certain areas, especially in my thought life. It never dawned on me until years later that Paul was not talking about behavior in this verse. He was talking about the new lives we have in Christ.

I am convinced that the majority of the family of faith falls into this same category. They keep failing in their walks of faith because they are trying to live their new lives in the ways they thought in their old lives. Many Christians are not even aware that they have a choice in how they think.

Being a new creation in Christ and still thinking the way we did before we were in Christ is a recipe for certain defeat. You can't live up to what you don't know you have. It is imperative that we bring our thinking in line with our identities. This is done by capturing our thoughts, renewing our minds, setting our thoughts on things above, and not allowing our feelings to get in the way. Living by faith is what pleases God, not feelings (Hebrews 11:6 NKJV). File this away in your memory bank: "Feelings are not fundamental to faith. Feelings can be fickle."

God Fills the Hearts of the Hungry

> Those who are hungry for him will always be filled,
> but the smug and self-satisfied he will send away
> empty. (Luke 1:53 TPT)

No food sounds good to a person who is not hungry. The individual who has become satisfied with normal Christianity and has no desire to know who they are and what they have in Christ will never experience reigning in this life—even though we were foreordained to do so (Romans 5:17 NKJV). Being more than a conqueror will only be a verse that has been memorized (Romans 8:37 NKJV). It will not be a living reality. Distance and delay will be their hope—someday they will conquer, someday they will reign—but until then, it is full-bore survival mode.

Luke says our hunger is to be for Jesus! When we come to really know Him, we begin to want what He wants, see things the way He sees them, think the way He thinks, and ultimately live our lives in total surrender to Him. When we die to ourselves and allow Christ to live His life through us, as us, we begin to live victorious lives.

Being Heavenly Minded Is the Only Way
We Can Be of Any Earthly Good

The vast majority of Christians have embraced Satan's egregious lie that it is possible to be so heavenly minded that we are of no earthly good, but being heavenly minded is the only way the body of Christ can be of any earthly good. I've heard people say, "Don't take this faith thing too far. If you do, you will become so heavenly minded you will be of no earthly good." Those words are usually spoken by Christians who have settled for normal Christianity. I am convinced that many, if not most, of these individuals are not even aware they have settled for a life that is so much less than what Christ has provided for them:

> For God made Christ, who never sinned, to be the offering for our sin, so that we could be made right with God through Christ. (2 Corinthians 5:21 NLT)

Let this verse get ahold of you. Jesus was willing to become what I was so I could be what He is (righteous).

During an emotional conversation concerning spiritual things, someone said, "What we need to be careful of is going too far with God." In response, the person they were talking to said, "It is impossible for you to go too far with God. As a matter of fact, you can't go far enough." They were quoting Smith Wigglesworth. Those words are spot-on. It is impossible to go too far with God. I have to admit that there was a time in my faith walk when I could have been the person who gave the warning against going too far with God. If we actually believe that it is possible to be so heavenly minded that we are no earthly good, this will be our position.

The unadulterated truth is that we are of little earthly good because we are not heavenly minded enough. This can be remedied by making the decision to walk away from being an average Christian.

However, as we have said several times already, it will take faith and a lot of courage. You will have people in your immediate circle of friends who think you have gone overboard in your faith. More than likely, you will be labeled as being weird or even more sinister: "one of those." They did that to Jesus, and believe me when I say that you will not receive a pass.

New Creation Identity Awakening

Can you imagine how devastating it would be to live your entire life as someone you were not—and not know your true identity until you were drawing your last breath. To make things even more shocking, you are made aware that the real you had incredible opportunities with unlimited resources at your fingertips. You were born into a royal family and were loved unconditionally, but you lived your whole life here on earth without knowing who you were or what you had.

I know that may sound strange, but it could be the autobiography of the vast majority of Christians. I have some incredible news for you, beloved. There is an identity awakening that is gaining momentum within the body of Christ. A lot of Christians are sick and tired of being sick and tired. There is hunger in the camp. These hungry hearts are being filled with the truth of the new creations Christ has made them to be. I am convinced that this move of the Spirit of God in the area of identity within the family of faith is to prepare us for this last season. A person would have to be asleep at the wheel not to know this world is spiraling out of control. If we don't bring our thinking in to line with our new creation identities, the chances of becoming casualties are tremendously enhanced. It is impossible for the new you (who you are in Christ) to live a victorious life if you try to live your new life by old you thinking (who you were before Christ). Old things have passed away, and all things have become new. That includes the ability to think differently (2 Corinthians 5:17 NKJV).

If we are going to impact this hurting, confused world with the love of God, it is imperative that we know who we are in Christ. To be of earthly good, we must be more heavenly minded than we have been. Remember that we can't go too far with God. If you don't believe me, try it.

It Is Time

It is time for us believers to do what we were designed and foreordained to do: reign in this life (Romans 5:17 NKJV). The way we think will determine whether reigning becomes a living reality or not. If we continue to think the way we did before we had our born-from-above experience with Christ, we will never reign. Until we do, this verse in Romans will only be black ink on a white page that is hidden away in our heads. It will never be a living reality in our hearts.

How do we begin? We start by believing whatever the Word of God says about our identities as new creations in Christ—even those passages that challenge our comfort zones, such as this one: "As He is, so are we in this world" (1 John 4:17 NKJV). That one verse alone is a game changer. That passage of scripture says that we are like Christ now—while we are in this world. What we think and how we feel about what this verse says does not affect or alter the truth of what God says about who we are in Him. The Spirit of God used 1 John 4:17 to activate an insatiable desire to know my new self identity. The last twenty-two years have been—and continue to be—the adventure of a lifetime. Every day, there is a new discovery. I believe it will continue until I make that transition from the seen realm into the unseen realm. Then I will know as I am known (1 Corinthians 13:12 NKJV).

The Lord has given me the opportunity to minister the exchanged life, new creation identity, to many pastors who were at their wits' end. They were tired, and many of them were on the verge of quitting the ministry. Some had quit. Here is the testimony of one of them. "I'm done." he told his wife. "Finished. I'm tired and frustrated. I will find me a job doing something, but I'm leaving the ministry."

She said, "Before you walk away from pastoring, please go see Wayne Kniffen in Hereford, Texas."

Because he loves his wife, he did what she asked him to do. When he heard about the exchanged life and his new creation self, his faith came alive. Burdens were lifted, and depression left as he began to soak in the truth about who Christ had made him to be. This was many years ago. Today, he is engaged in ministry like never before. His personal life is filled with rest, and his ministry life is filled with freedom. The Lord is now using him to help other pastors get free, help the people they shepherd get free, and stay free. When the Lord sets a person free, they are free indeed (John 8:36 NKJV). It is one thing to be free, but it is another thing to be free indeed. This is why new creation thinking is so crucial to living as more than conquerors and reigning in this life.

I have spent many hours with discouraged Christians who were on the brink of throwing in the towel. They had burned themselves out by working hard to become what they already were. When a person gets to this state in their faith walk, they are left with a few options. They can quit, and many do, or start pretending they are okay when they are not. There is a third option. They can make the decision to walk away from being a normal Christian. Doing this will take faith and a lot of courage, but it will be the best decision of their lives since they accepted and received Jesus Christ as their Lord and Savior.

Whatever you do, don't settle for a life that does not measure up to the new creation identity you have been gifted with. It is time to start thinking like new creation beings. When this happens, we will begin to live our lives from the inside out.

ABOUT THE AUTHOR

Wayne Kniffen is a gifted speaker and writer. He has the ability to communicate complex spiritual truths in ways that most people can understand. Kniffen is quick-witted and uses humor to keep his audience alert. He often says, "I have learned that people will swallow more truth if they can laugh it down."

Kniffen has been a senior pastor for almost fifty years. Writing has become his passion in this final season of his life. He continues to serve as a senior pastor. For twenty-seven years, he served churches in East Texas, and for the past twenty-three years, he has pastored in West Texas. He says, "Pastoring in East Texas is who I was, but pastoring in West Texas is who I am." When he exchanged East Texas for West Texas, he discovered his true new creation identity.

Other available books by Kniffen are *The Scam*, which deals with Satan's attempt to steal our new creation identities, and *The Exchange: God's Quid Pro Quo*. *The Exchange* deals with how we receive our new creation identities. *If We Only Knew* exposes the truth about ignorance. Ignorance may not be bliss. *The Prodigal: Seen Through the Eyes of the Father* goes into great detail about how God sees us, feels about us, and thinks about us. *New Creation Thinking* zeroes in on our thought lives and how we think should coincide with the new creations Christ has made us to be. All books were published by WestBow Press and are available from many outlets. More of Kniffen's books will be released in the near future, including *Spiritual COVID*, *The Power of Releasing*, *My Proverbs*, *Thirty-Two*

Women, When God Breathes, The Fish That Caught a Man, and *Aha Moments with Jesus.*

The author can be contacted by e-mail at WayneKniffen@ outlook.com.

Printed in the United States
by Baker & Taylor Publisher Services